# The Secret Key
# To The Moors Murders

# The Secret Key
# To The Moors Murders

*Erica Gregory*

authorHOUSE®

*AuthorHouse™ UK Ltd.*
*1663 Liberty Drive*
*Bloomington, IN 47403 USA*
*www.authorhouse.co.uk*
*Phone: 0800.197.4150*


© *2013 by Erica Gregory. All rights reserved.*

*No part of this book may be reproduced, stored in a retrieval system, or transmitted by any means without the written permission of the author.*

*Published by AuthorHouse    10/02/2013*

*ISBN: 978-1-4918-8072-2 (sc)*
*ISBN: 978-1-4918-8073-9 (e)*

*Any people depicted in stock imagery provided by Thinkstock are models, and such images are being used for illustrative purposes only.*
*Certain stock imagery © Thinkstock.*


*Because of the dynamic nature of the Internet, any web addresses or links contained in this book may have changed since publication and may no longer be valid. The views expressed in this work are solely those of the author and do not necessarily reflect the views of the publisher, and the publisher hereby disclaims any responsibility for them.*

# FOREWORD

If you enter any true crime bookstore whether real or virtual you will encounter a number of books about Myra Hindley, Ian Brady and the 'Moors Murders'. Most of these books are written by people who never knew either of the perpetrators or their victims and use Hindley's iconic 'Medusa' police photograph on the cover almost as a guaranteed stamp of mediocrity. It was therefore with some caution that I approached this new book on the subject.

However I could not have been more wrong and was delighted to discover that this volume offers a very fresh perspective which, most importantly, is prepared to take some of the *risks* which previous authors have usually shied away from.

The text presents intriguing new insights mainly from two related themes:

Firstly, the contributors are resident in the area of the murder cycle, both at the time of the murders and the decades since. In this respect they are able to authentically gauge the shocking personal impact that these terrible murders have had on almost everyone who became associated with them, people who knew the victims or were simply living within the geographical vicinity of the crimes.

Secondly, they have attempted to integrate an encyclopaedic analysis of challenging literary and philosophical sources into a fascinating quest to reveal the foundations of the criminal inspiration behind the crimes. Drawing on authors such as Joyce, Chaucer, Shakespeare, Dante and others, all of which Brady was highly familiar with, they lead us through a labyrinth of possibilities. Like any maze, some of the pathways and clues just lead to further clues but the reader does not find this frustrating as this allows opportunities to embark on alternative doors of possibility. Whether such an approach will ultimately lead to the discovery of the remains of Keith Bennett or indeed any other of Brady and Hindley's victims remains to be seen but there is no doubt that this is a fascinating text which expands and enlightens the scope of inquiry into what many regard as one of the most notorious crimes in British criminal history.

Dr Chris Cowley (Author of 'Face to Face with Evil: Conversations with Ian Brady')

May, 2013

**Special thanks:**

Thank you to everyone who has helped and supported us throughout—and to those who helped us search the Moors.

We greatly appreciate the special efforts made by the people who volunteered their own time and energy to do extensive research into the Moors Murders.

# FACT OR FICTION?

## THE KEY TO THE MOORS MURDERS?

BRADY'S LIFE ............................................................... 1
HINDLEY'S LIFE ........................................................ 10
JAMES JOYCE'S LIFE ................................................ 20
JAMES JOYCE'S WORK ............................................. 25
BRADY VS JOYCE ...................................................... 99
MYRA VS MOLLY ..................................................... 119
PAULINE READE'S STORY ..................................... 126
JOHN KILBRIDE'S STORY ..................................... 138
KEITH BENNETT'S STORY ................................... 152
LESLEY ANN DOWNEY'S STORY ......................... 157
EDWARD EVAN'S STORY ....................................... 164
IMPORTANT DATES AND CONNECTIONS
   FOR THE CHILDREN ......................................... 172
FOOD FOR THOUGHT ........................................... 202
THE SOUTH ............................................................. 210
LINKS TO DIFFERENT AREAS .............................. 222
ALL OTHER LINKS ................................................. 237
CONCLUSION ......................................................... 294

Ever wondered what really goes on in the mind of a serial killer?

What drove Ian Brady to his crimes?

Have we discovered Brady's hidden code? Our extensive research into these murders may have given us something others may have overlooked.

Was Myra Hindley a genuine victim of Brady's ideas as she has previously stated? Was she just his partner in crime? Perhaps she may have taken it a step further.
Brady told David Smith he was making a "Story to impress". He wasn't making a story, he was living it.

In this book, we believe we may hold the true answers to the endless questions circling this brutal case.


This book is to help fill in the gaps missed by others. With discussion as to how they avoided detection for such a long time and how they acted both inside and outside of prison.

Myra managed to deceive many people, including journalists—by altering how the public perceived her, Myra saw this as a method to aid her freedom.
She forced the public into thinking Brady was manipulating her by making her diaries a "Mills and Boon Novel" based on her and Brady.
Perhaps Myra was being manipulated; but only at the beginning. Myra soon became as strong as her partner. When caught, Myra refused to give any answers regarding the whereabouts of victims. She used quotes as cryptic messages—continuing to play a sick game until the day she died.

# ABOUT US—WORSLEY PARANORMAL GROUP

The work of Worsley Paranormal Group includes research into discovering any missing or unnamed victims of Ian Brady and Myra Hindley. This has been difficult but worthwhile work for the members.

Worsley Paranormal Group was founded in 2005. The main members of the group are Erica Gregory and her husband Paul (Founders), working together with her sisters, Lesley McCormack, Tracy Reed-Goodehall, Kim Edgington and their mum Margaret Reed. They also have a larger group field which includes Erica and Paul's son, daughter and friends—they assist the investigations in larger areas.

The Worsley Paranormal Group began two years after their dad died on January 2$^{nd}$ 2003 (coincidentally this is also Ian Brady's birthday).

He died after a sudden illness; and this was a terrible shock to the family and especially for their mum.

Soon after his death, strange things occurred in the home of Margaret to which no one could explain: smells of smoke and tobacco despite nobody smoking. Noises and feelings occurred which made the family feel as though their dad was trying to get through to them. Erica wanted a form of evidence that would assure her their dad was well; she wanted to know if there was some form of life after death.

This is when Erica decided that she would create her own paranormal group, to investigate different areas for evidence of potential life after death.

After taking a Diploma in Paranormal Investigation she studied the work of famous investigators. The investigators are not mediums, nor are the members of Worsley Paranormal Group—instead they use various devices which are widely available for anyone to use.

They noticed that by using voice recorders they were picking up EVPs (Electronic Voice Phenomenon)—this was discovered during an investigation in 2006 at Smithills Hall in Bolton. As the voices they picked up were so strong, the group invested in more recorders (Normal Olympus VN recorders—used for general recording). More EVPs were heard on the recorders during the investigations at various locations.

This led the main group to begin investigating homes for people with claims of paranormal activity. EVPs were being picked up at the majority of places investigated. This provoked them to question that maybe there is more to life after death which nobody yet fully understands.

Voices were giving names and responding to questions. Some of these are so clear that it sounds like there are people sat in the room with them—others are quiet and distant. They were finding physical evidence that the claims made by the home owners were accurate. The group continue to investigate different homes and areas.

Erica has studied EVP for many years now, and has a greater understanding of the paranormal field.

The group never expected to be going to Saddleworth Moor.

Erica practices EVPs at home with the recorder and on one particular occasion in 2011, Erica heard words sounding like "Saddleworth" and "sheep pen". She uploaded them to the group's Facebook page.

A psychic medium who had herself been to the Moors many times—contacted Erica . . . Christine Hamlet-Walsh, came to visit the Group in 2011 she made arrangements to take them to the areas the children were found—this was a first for the group.

On the 5th November they visited the area of John Kilbride's grave, Rimmon pit cottage and Hollins Brown knoll.

On their first visit they found bones in a direct West position buried under rocks not far from John's grave. The police were informed and came up to the moor to take the bones away. They were sheep bones and had been placed in an area close to a Druid burial ground. After going back home that day, another EVP was found on the recorders.

From this, the group researched the Moors Murders and decided they were meant to assist. EVPs were captured which were linked to the Moors. All of their work is online to view.

On a 3rd visit to the moors they found the shovel buried near a stream in a shale embankment.

Many more items and symbols have also been found in the same area—SOUTH of the other children.

The rest is explained in the book.

Erica would like to add: "The EVPs have assisted my study and research. I feel I have been helped along to find evidence on this case that others may have missed.

We hope that we have brought in the missing pieces of this puzzle that so many have not understood.

As for my work, I don't try and make others believe, we all have our own views on the Paranormal, just as with religion and other beliefs. But if our work can help to bring an end to something and bring peace to all the families involved then that is what will make us happy.

We have dedicated the past 16 months to this. I myself have worked on books, films and art—things that I had no idea about before. I wanted to come into the case seeing it through Brady's eyes—by looking the things closest to him and that was his beloved books.

The books they hid in the suitcases, on bookshelves and also given to each other as a code at the trial."

She also adds: "Ian Brady's book published in 2001—The Gates of Janus—is also how we have researched specific areas on the Moors. We started to see a pattern forming with the dates the children were murdered.

By researching the lives of the poets Brady quoted within Janus, I was able to see certain poets fitting in with dates used for each child.

I have spent 12 months deciphering Janus and what myself and the group have found are snippets of what Brady has done himself within his writings of other serial killers.

He quotes things in 'Janus' which seem to resemble landmarks in the area we are searching. We have found many items, not just the shovel. The group have used their own time and resources; we have been back to the area many times and also to visit other significant places. This enables us to see it from a different point of view.

I hope that the public will see this also".

We sincerely hope that Keith Bennett and the other forgotten victims can soon be laid to rest.

Worsley Paranormal Group UK.

## Timeline of finds:

**November 5th 2011**—First visit. The discovery of the sheep bones buried under a rock in a West point position not far from where John Kilbride was found. They informed the police, who marked the area and removed the bones. They were sheep bones. Erica then kept in touch with Oldham CID. She came to realise that 'The Gates of Janus mentioned Keith Bennett in a cryptic way-after this she put in contact with the cold case team at Ashton.

The chapter of the Hillside Strangler at the end of the book mentions how a KB brings back memories. She then began sending her findings to the police.

This book should have been dealt with in 2001.

**11th November 2011 and 13th November 2011**—They went back to Saddleworth to have a look at an area South of the other children, which Lesley had highlighted by using Google Earth.

They noted the 3 children had been buried to the North, West and East. This made sense to the group, there could be other victims buried in the South.

Anyone who has studied serial killers will know they keep a pattern.

They found that going towards the South from the top moor was very dangerous. They continued to search for an easier route to reach the South.

Brady quoted in Janus the "Two" by W H Auden. This poem is very descriptive of a Greenfield and there being two of everything.

They found from the maps in the South there are two waterfalls, two weirs, two streams and a rock formation facing the area known as the 'Two Trinnacles'. Everything in that area is of TWO. They found by parking at Binn Greene, they could walk to the area easier. On this walk you would pass Ashway Gap, a Gothic house that Brady and Hindley visited. The area of the pine woods where many photos of the pair with rifles were taken. So they decided South was a good spot to check and made arrangements to go on the 20th November.

**20th November 2011**—They visited the area South as planned. Erica had re-searched more and found that in Janus, Brady made references to Dante. She researched Dante and The Divine Comedy—a trip to purgatory was in hand.

In the book of the Divine Comedy, she found purgatory was South. She also found the Southern Crux—a star formation—which revolves anti-clockwise in the sky.

So this gives strength to the idea of the anti-clockwise burial of the children. This appears as an upside down cross if viewed from Hollins Brown Knoll—another reference to Satan.

This was the day they uncovered the shovel.

Lesley had done extensive research into the area. She had looked at many pictures on the internet and using Google Earth and satellite images, she had an accurate idea of the landscape and where the search would begin.

When they arrived at the area, Lesley noted the two trinnacles and an Oak tree which had been discussed as a checkpoint. Paul climbed down a small hill to the stream bed with a metal detector in hand; they all felt this was an important place. Within a few minutes of searching, under a crag, buried in shale, was the shovel.

Erica telephoned the police and reported the find—a shock to everyone was, the police were not interested, telling them to leave it and they would collect the shovel when they were next in the area. However, they did not leave it. They put the shovel into a plastic bag and marked the area—this was later handed to the police.

A meeting with locals and landowners confirmed the area they are investigating has never been searched by the police or search teams previously.

They visited a few times over the winter to check the stream bed, but the weather was against them.

They began studying the Moors case in more depth, and soon came to realise 'The Gates of Janus' could hold a cryptic message giving clues regarding the murders.

**March 2012**—Taking notes of quotes written and spoken by Brady and Hindley, they felt the following important:-

Myra quoted 'Like a lamb to the slaughter'

The area contains 'The Lamb stones' and Lamb knoll.

Three of the group members climbed up to the Lamb Stones and came across a Split oak tree, a plateau area and a stone sheep-pen. They saw these as possible markers. The group members then decided to walk to the road, an experiment to discover how accessible this route could have been for a boy with no glasses. They dismissed the possibility as this route was far too dangerous.

The path from an area known as Ashway Gap was much more suitable.

A very clear EVP was picked up at Erica's home saying 'Brady's spade",

Having learnt the shovel was now simply sitting in a cupboard at the police station, they requested it back from the police and managed to find a forensic scientist to do some testing—the tests were to take several months.

They also decided it was time to send their findings to Ashworth Hospital including photos of the site—in a hope of provoking some kind of response from Brady which the staff there could witness

**April 2012**—During this search they found a symbol on a rock resembling a triangle. This reminded them of a Pagan symbol, or even Masonic. Erica had been studying rock carvings in literature, medievalism and mythology in the month leading up to this search. She had a feeling they would find something—still being shocked when they did. During a closer inspection and after more research at home, she realised it also resembled a map. Erica has sent all the information to Cold Case.

She also started to write to Ian Brady to inform him she was studying The Gates of Janus and the poetry he quoted within his writing. Erica felt he needed to take this on board. She wanted him to know the area was being searched—again hoping to provoke a response.

Through Erica's research of James Joyce's life and the discovery of a photograph of Myra sitting over a broken tree with the initials FW carved into it—she questioned if this could stand for Finnegan's Wake. This is a book which mentions trees, stones and resurrection. This is explained in more detail later in the book. Ian Brady knows about all of their findings but has never responded.

The group didn't go to the Moors much during the summer as the weather made it difficult to search. On the few occasions they did go it was with a small group of friends who were a great help with the physically demanding digs.

On one such visit they noted a Rock which resembled a lion head. Paul stated the area with the Lamb knoll and stones reminded him of the Lake District—the area of Grasmere where Wordsworth and the Lake poets lived. Brady and Hindley visited the Lakes many times.

**September 2012**

The group had a meeting with the family of one of the victims and shared their findings.

A Newspaper article about the shovel was printed in September.

Erica had contacted a criminologist; for advice. He felt the shovel needed to be investigated further so in a hope of raising awareness and hopefully finding support, it was agreed the story should be printed.

No payment was accepted by anyone involved in this story.

Also during this month a chance meeting on the Moors led to a new member joining the group.

**October visit 2012**—The group returned to the Moors accompanied by a family member of one of the victims

Ryan, an archaeologist, has helped the group several times with their searches, and his knowledge has been invaluable, and also new member—Margaret.

On this visit they decided to investigate the split Oak tree area properly.

This led to the discovery of more bones; they were the bones of a sheep buried in a South position at the base of the tree. The bones were taken and dated by an anthropologist. They were from two post-mortem cut sheep; again buried under a rock. If this is a pattern then a body may not be far from here with a burial similar to John's.

**November 2012**—This month the group visited Gorton cemetery. They had been directed here by a lady interested in the case. She wanted us to examine the Statue next to Michael Higgins grave. The statue is described later and they saw something others hadn't.

They cleaned up Michael's grave and found a shoe buried down under an old stump which was removed. Much of the shoe had been destroyed but parts of a cheap leather material were found. They knew from their research that John Kilbride had a shoe missing.

Back on the Moors the following week they discovered tins, cans and a fork—these were buried by the stream bed directly below the area of the sheep-pen and the tree.

With winter getting closer, the group did more research and visited a grave at St James' Church. There was evidence that something may have been buried there. A witness had reported seeing Ian Brady bury something in this grave. It wasn't reported to the police until 2011 as yet nothing has been done. The name on the grave is important—that name would have attracted Brady. Yet again this links to literature and poetry—the date 16th June is part of this.

The group also visited Stalybridge. This is explained later in the book, but they do have a very good reason as to why Myra had her ashes scattered there.

**April, May & June 2013**—Removed Brady's hells door, the split tree—this is from research into books like Dante and Celtic history.

They also felt the sheep pen needed further investigation—their findings shocked them, buried a foot or so below the ground they discovered: a crude cross made from wood which had been tied together with rope and red electrical flex.

After this the group went back for a few more visits with others to help. What they have found to date is a large amount of polythene (the majority of this had been burnt), a burnt part of a plastic shoe (this had been wrapped in a white wire ligature), a clump of knotted rope, signs of a fire and a large amount of ash covered by the rocks.

On June 16th they discovered more bones, they now know are animal.

The bones were taken to be tested in a lab. A group member received news of the results, she was informed that although the bones are animal they were showing traces of human DNA.

The bones may have been buried near to, or been in contact with human DNA, possibly from within the peat itself. This showed signs that the soil may be contaminated.

They continued their visits to the Moors to gather more evidence.

*Erica Gregory*

The group felt they had gathered enough evidence for the area to be searched. Alas this is not the case; further evidence is needed before the police will assist them in a thorough search.

Ian Brady spent so much time planning his areas. He pinpointed the burials with the use of a compass and map. The symbol on the rock of an esoteric triangle shows this.

All items are shown in the book and many items found, link to literature and poetry.

All of the items were found in an area never searched by the police. If they find another victim here this can only be a good thing.

To find the victims you need to know which story was acted out and why.

# EPISODE 1

O, what a tangled web we weave when first we practise to deceive!
                                                    Walter Scott

## Ian Brady's Background.

---

On the 2nd January 1938, Peggy Stewart became an unmarried mother.

At Rottenrow Maternity Hospital, Glasgow, she gave birth to a healthy 8lb little boy who she named Ian Stewart. Ian's dad was an unknown reporter for a Glasgow newspaper who apparently died 3 months before the birth of the boy. Peggy never revealed the name of Ian's father for reasons unknown.

At the time of Ian's birth, Peggy was living with a friend at 8 Huntingdon Place in a rundown, poverty stricken part of Glasgow. Once Peggy and baby Ian returned home from hospital it was apparent that they were not welcome—mainly due to the bad criticism of being an unmarried mother.

Peggy was forced to find alternative accommodation for herself and the baby. She found a place in Caledonia Road, Gorbals, which was more rundown than the previous place, however it was a place they could call their own—a place she could call home.

To financially support herself, and Ian, Peggy returned to her previous job as a part-time tearoom waitress. Unfortunately this meant Peggy had to leave young Ian for hours at a time with young girls (consisting of mostly neighbours) to babysit him. While Peggy was away from Ian she was constantly worried about him and always felt relieved when she returned home to find him safe and well.

After a while Peggy realised she could not carry on with the way things were. She believed that she was not doing everything she could for her son despite her best efforts.

After a lot of soul searching she came to the heart-breaking decision that Ian would be better off if he were brought up by another family. That way they could give him everything she couldn't.

Peggy decided to put out an advert saying "working widow willing to have son adopted". Peggy did not hold out any hope at getting a response and was very shocked when a few days later she was contacted by a lady called Mary Sloan.

Mary was in her 40's with very bad hearing. Peggy met with Mary and her husband John Sloan—after some time talking and thinking on both sides it was decided that Ian would go and live with the Sloan's.

The Sloan's already had 4 children—two boys and 2 girls—all were older than Ian. Peggy believed Ian would be better living with a settled family who could give him the attention and care that she could not.

At 4 months old, Peggy pushed her curly, fair haired and deep grey eyed little boy in his rundown silver cross pram for the final time. She arrived at 56 Camden Street which would be Ian's new home.

Arrangements were made for Peggy to visit her son as often as she wanted. Usually being a Sunday, she would bring Ian little presents or treats. Ian refers to Peggy now as Aunt Peggy.

The Sloan's house was facing Southern Necropolis Cemetery; the cemetery had wide paths and was a peaceful place. Mary Sloan spent many hours pushing Ian round the paths in his pram.

Peggy continued to visit until Ian was 12 years of age; this is when she moved to Manchester with her new husband Patrick Brady who she has recently married.

On the 3rd September 1939, the Second World War broke out. Ian at this time was at the tender age of one year and eight months old. The war finished when he was seven and a half years old. The war didn't impact major changes to the people living in Glasgow. This was due to the men who were called up for duty being paid more money than in their everyday jobs. Even the rationing did not affect Mary Sloan as she was used to feeding her family on a low income.

At the age of five, Ian went to Camden Street Primary School. Ian was seen as an independent, intelligent young boy. He learned to read and write quicker than any other child in his year group. However, there was another side to Ian—if he was cross, got shouted at or did not get his own way he would throw massive tantrums often resulting in him banging his head against a cushion and growling till he was red in the face.

Ian's favourite topic at school was learning about King Arthur and the Knights of the Round Table, as well as the other topics that associated with them such as castles and dungeons.

Ian became a big film fanatic and made lists of all the films he saw, both these things would become significant in later life as you will discover from reading this book.

It is believed that Ian's love of wide open Moor land spaces came from a trip Ian took with the Sloan family when he was younger.

The family visited Loch Lomond for one of his foster sibling's birthday to have a family day of fun and a picnic. After lunch the family dozed off in the afternoon sun. When they woke they found young Ian gone, he was stood high above them on a hill side gazing intently around at the wide open beauty spot and the Loch beneath him. It took a considerable time for the family to coax Ian down from the hill for their return trip home.

After the trip, Ian never spoke of it again to the Sloan's, or spoke about what he had been thinking about.

In 1947 the Sloan's moved from their home in the Gorbals, to a more up market address at 21 Templland Road. This was on an overspill estate three miles from Pollok. The house was a nice two story, semi-detached house with an indoor bathroom and garden. It was located near a golf course and open countryside.

Ian was thought to be a very intelligent child and passed his entrance exams to Shawlands Academy. Shawlands was seen as one of the best schools in the area. Mr and Mrs Sloan were very proud of young Ian's achievements. Their joy however was short lived as Ian started to become very lazy and uninterested in his school work or activities.

It was speculated that Ian bullied other children and was known for his perverse and sadistic tendencies. There were rumours of Ian torturing animals; there is a story about him locking a cat away to see how long it would take for it to starve to death. Ian denies all stories of animal cruelty stating that he loves animals more than he loves people.

Ian left Shawlands academy at the age of 15 and took a job as a tea boy at a Harland and Wolff shipyard in Govan.

Nine months later he began working as a butcher's messenger boy. He had a girlfriend, Evelyn Grant, but their relationship broke down when he threatened her with a flick knife after she visited a dance with another boy.

In time, Ian became involved with crime, starting off with small robberies and then progressed into breaking into houses—most likely doing this to support his habit of smoking. On the first two occasions of being in court on the same charges, he got off lightly with probation but soon returned to his life of crime. On the third time before a judge he was deemed in correctable. Instead of being sent to a juvenile centre he was ordered to go and live with his maternal mother, Peggy. Previously stated she had married an Irish man named Patrick Brady and moved to Manchester to be with her husband.

So in November 1954, Ian aged 16 left the Sloan Family and Scotland behind him. He moved in with his mother and step-father in an area of Manchester known as Moss Side—the address 13A Denmark Street, which was to say the least, no better of an area from where he had moved from in Glasgow.

Ian took his step-father's surname to be known as Ian Stewart Brady. Unfortunately the new name and new area did not bring about a new Brady. He could have had a chance to restart his life but he decided crime was the life for him. Ian was not fond of dead end jobs for minimum wage.

Brady's stepfather got him a job as a fruit porter at Smith-field Market in Gorton, Manchester. This is also where his stepfather worked.

Within a year of Brady's move to Manchester, Brady was caught with a 44 pound sack full of lead seals that he had stolen—he was caught trying to smuggle them out of the market.

He was sentenced to two years in Borstal, for 'training' but spent the first 3 months in Strangeways prison Manchester, this was until a space could be found for him at a young offenders prison.

Having spent time in an adult prison, Brady was sent to Latchmere house in London, and then Hatfield borstal in Yorkshire. However after he was discovered intoxicated on alcohol he had brewed himself, he was moved to a much tougher unit at Hull.

Brady was released on 14th November 1957 and returned to Manchester. His parents were now living temporarily at 97 Grey Mare Lane.

Once he arrived back in Manchester he took a labouring job which he hated and this was soon dismissed for another job at Boddingtons Brewery. His stepfather would often make sly remarks to Peggy about the job being good for Brady due to it being located next door to Strangeways Prison.

Patrick Brady had lost all interest and faith in his step-son after he made a laughing stock out of him when he stole from Smithfield market. The job at the brewery lasted for five months before Brady was made redundant. Patrick Brady made a comment: "well better to be made redundant than for the job to end with him being in the docks".

Ian decided to "better himself", he obtained a set of instruction manuals on book-keeping from a local public library, which he studied alone in his room for hours this "astonished" his parents.

On the 2nd February (this date is important, publication of Ulysses 1922 by James Joyce) in 1959 Brady applied for and was offered a clerical job at Mill Wards Merchandising. This was a wholesale chemical distribution company based in Gorton.

Brady's step-father being ever critical of his step-son told him he did not know how to hold a job down. He was very surprised when Brady stayed in this employment for six years and two hundred and thirty two days. The reason the employment ended was due to his eventual arrest for the murder of Edward Evans. He was regarded by his work colleagues as a quiet and punctual lad but was also short tempered.

During his lunch breaks he would read books such as teach yourself German, Mein Kampf; he would also study poets.

Brady had also started taking an interest in the bookies—especially the horses—and many of his dinner breaks he could be seen fluttering between his books and the bookies.

Not too long after the move to Grey Mare Lane the family was on the move again, this time to 18 Westmoreland Street. This was a little over a mile away from their old address. (Much found about Ian Brady's early life can be linked to our findings to date).

When Brady wasn't at work he could be found in his bedroom reading books such like "The Kiss of the Whip". His libraries of books were very eclectic and not the usual books a young man in Manchester would read to say the least. However, if only people could have realised just how much reading these books have influenced his life and the 'road ahead' he took.

# EPISODE 2

"Keith went like a lamb to the Slaughter"
Quote Myra Hindley

## Myra Hindley's background

Myra Hindley was born on Thursday 23rd July 1942, to parents Nellie and Bob Hindley.

She was conceived mid-Second World War while Bob Hindley was on home leave from his Parachute Regiment.

By the time war was over she was the tender age of 3 years old and was classed a very well behaved child and loved by all that knew her—especially Granny Maybury. She lived around the corner from the Hindley's at 24 Beasley Street, back to back with her street. Myra spent as much time with her Granny as she did at home with her parents. Not only was Granny close to them, other family members also lived within a close proximity.

Nellie's half brother Jim Burn's lived with his wife 4 miles away in Dukinfield; her brother Bert Maybury lived with his family in Clayton not even a mile away from their home at 20 Eaton Street Gorton, Greater Manchester.

On 21st August 1946, Hindley's younger sister Maureen was born. Hindley doted on her younger sister;

After Maureen was born their family adapted a new way of life—this was later misunderstood by others outside of the family. It most likely seemed that young Hindley was being pushed out of her family due to the birth of her sister. The situation was Myra was packed off to live with her Grandma in the next street: the classic example of the rejected child storing up fatal resentments?

One of the stories was the arrival of a second child meant: "the house was not big enough". This was seen as strange in a community where families housed four or five children at a time. Therefore for two young girls to share a back bedroom together would not have been seen as over-crowding.

What actually happened was that Mrs Maybury (Myra's Grandmother) absolutely adored her three year old granddaughter Myra and begged Nellie and Bob to allow Myra to go and live with her; the grandmother was a lonely widow who was still in her fifties.

Nellie was desperate to get her job back as a machinist as her husband was unable to work. The thought of working and caring for two young children was a very hard situation. Mrs Maybury living so close to the family made it easier for the family and so it did not really feel like Myra was moving away from them.

The move went ahead with Myra moving in to 24 Beasley Street with her grandmother. Myra loved being with her Gran and she loved having her there.

The next year, Mrs Maybury moved—but only next door to number 22. This was later followed by another move to number 7; by the time of the second move Beasley Street had been renamed Bannock Street.

The move did not affect young Myra in the slightest; she spent equal amounts of time at Eaton Street with her parents and sister as she did at Bannock Street with her Gran. Due to the houses being virtually backed on to each other she could easily slip from one house to the other. Not only were the houses so close together but both houses were also identical in their lay out and even the furniture, even some of the photographs in the parlour were identical.

It was an easy-going way of life, but definitely not conductive to instability.

Myra was a healthy young girl who always ate and slept well. Myra was a very determined little girl who absolutely adored her young sister. At aged 5 Myra nicknaming her sister Baby-Mo then Mo-Baby and as the time went on she started calling her Mo-Bee, this nickname stayed with her until her death.

Myra was very protective of her young sister and there was never once a question of any jealousy towards her. The situation with young Myra living between two houses was not all perfect. Gran was a gentle, kind and caring woman.

Gran's main goal in life was to run a clean and happy home for herself and Myra—this was to ensure the young girl could spend her time being a child and enjoy her childhood. However, Nellie had other ideas as to how she wanted Myra to learn; how to become a good house-wife, doing the cooking, cleaning and sewing etc. In the days of young Myra's youth it was believed women should do this. They must stay at home and ensure their husbands came home from work or the pub to a clean house, tea cooked and quiet children.

Due to her Gran's lack of discipline, Myra began to take her for granted. As a young girl Myra got on very well with other children she would often be seen playing in the street or on wasteland. She would often play tag and enjoyed playing games on a field. When she came home all dirty and clothes ripped, she would stamp about and have tantrums when Gran insisted she got changed and cleaned herself up. Often due to her refusing Gran would have to forcibly clean young Myra, she was a typical tom-boy.

At age 5, Myra started school at Peacock Street County Primary, the school was a few minutes' walk from either her Gran's house or her parent's house—it was located on Gorton Lane.

Myra's parents were delighted when at the age of 11 it came to their attention that Myra was considered intelligent enough to attend secondary school. This was considered very good for a girl at that time as most young girls were bought up knowing their duty in adulthood would be to become a good housewife and mother. The secondary school in which Myra attended was named Ryder Brow. It was located about a mile from where she lived.

Ryder Brow was seen as one of the schools that could take a girl from any background and turn them into a teacher, nurse or a political leader. Myra was a good student especially at Maths and English, one of her assignments at school was to choose a subject and write a story about it: Myra chose to write about a ship-wreck. Her story was apparently so good that it was bound and placed in the library for all to see and read; Myra was extremely pleased about this.

Myra walked the mile to and from school all the time. Her family recall that every time Myra took this walk there were two places she would always stop and admire with fascination: first was on her right by Glencastle Road. There was a little church of the sacred heart Gorton, three statues high over the door with Christ dying on the cross—beside him, a disciple and his mother. Myra often made comments about how sad it made her feel and what a horrible way to die it must have been. On her left was Sunny Brow Park—it had a miniature lake and a foot high dwarf waterfall. Each day she passed Myra would mutter the same mantra as she passes: 'morning thou sacred heart, morning thou waterfall'.

Myra joined in nearly every physical activity available at school. She was a good fielder at rounders, an excellent defender during netball and she was also a strong swimmer. Her Gran had a picture of young Myra with the rest of her gym class looking happy and giddy down the camera.

Due to Gran's lenient ways Myra had an unsatisfactory attendance at school; it was due to this that she failed her 11+ exams despite being an above average pupil with the IQ of 109.

In the summer of 1957 it was the end of the summer term at school and the end of Myra's education. At the age of 15, Myra was not picked out as one of those pupils who could stay on at school and look at continuing onto university. Now she left school to get a job which would be seen as her way as helping out financially in the family home.

When Hindley was nearly fifteen years old she was seen as a fiery outspoken kind of girl. She would be the one to light up a cigarette on a bus when she was not allowed— or if one of her friends was being bullied, she would be the one to stick up for them. She was feared by many of her fellow school pupils.

Hindley shocked a lot of people when she befriended a 13 year old boy named Michael Higgins. Being the complete opposite to Hindley he was a quiet, shy young boy and was often on the receiving end of bully's taunts.

Michael and his family were devoted Catholics and attended mass every Sunday without fail. Hindley and Michael's friendship was very strong even though she was at the time dating Ronnie Woodcock. After a while they became engaged—however, now she had started work she decided she did not want the life of a housewife: cooking, cleaning and looking after children. She ended her relationship with him.

Michael began to come out of his shell when he was around Myra and together they would sneak through the fencing at Belle Vue Speedway as they could not afford to go any other way. Hindley's other Nana 'Kitty' worked at the speedway so Hindley would approach the racers enclosure pretending her Nan had sent her and she would beg the drivers for autographs for Michael's collection.

On the 14th June 1957 the locals were enjoying an extremely hot summers day whilst watching the annual whit parade. Hindley was one of the spectators stood on the pavement cheering and clapping. Michael was lucky enough to have been chosen to carry one of the banners and Hindley was so proud of Michael—she had a big smile on her face during the parade.

Hindley was with a couple of her friends Pat Jepson and Pat's sister Barbara. Once the parade was over Michael asked Hindley if she wanted to go swimming with him in the nearby Gorton Reservoir. Despite the fact Hindley enjoyed swimming and was extremely good she declined Michael's offer—she had already made plans to go to Pat and Barbara's Auntie's house in Reddish for tea.

On their way back, Hindley stood on the back platform of the bus to get some fresh air. She suddenly she saw a young boy pedalling furiously to catch up with the bus shouting at the three girls. They jumped down off the platform to see what the commotion was about. He breathlessly started to say there had been an accident at the reservoir in Mellands Fields. Hindley did not let the young lad finish his sentence she set of running as fast as she could through the streets of Gorton—racing to get there.

As she approached the field there were several people walking her way, one member of the crowd broke away to go and answer Hindley's high-pitch cry for answers.

Michael had gone swimming with Eddie Hogan and a boy younger than the pair—named Walter King. They had been swimming all afternoon and Michael had dived into the water with another boy. Unlike the other, Michael did not surface.

The boys kept diving in to see if they could see Michael but they could not. A bystander alerted the police and within minutes the police were swarming all over the area—teamed with fire-fighters and paramedics. The reservoir varied in depth from 10ft to 25ft. It remained chillingly cold even during the height of summer.

Grappling lines were brought in and Michael's parents were notified.

It was 6:50pm when a Lancashire County Frogman emerged causing ripples on the surface of the water, the crowd went silent and Hindley and Michael's parents held their breath. He came out of the water carrying the grey, cold, limp body of poor Michael.

They hurriedly put him in the mortuary van and Michael's mum stumbled to the ambulance to be with the body of her 13 year old son. Hindley was hysterical and screaming—saying it was all her fault. She said she should not have left him to go for tea. She believed because she was such a strong swimmer she could have saved him.

Hindley begged her mother to make her a black hair band as a sign of respect; she visited door to door collecting money for a funeral wreath. Mrs Higgins was touched by how much she had cared for Michael. She could see how much Myra was grieving for him—for that she gave her Michael's speedway programmes which Hindley had helped to collect. Everybody else thought there was something wrong with the way Hindley was grieving.

On the day of Michael's funeral Mrs Higgins invited Hindley into the house to see his Michael laid out in the coffin—to bid farewell. Mrs Higgins thought it would help her find peace.

Mrs Higgins slipped the rosary beads from his hand and placed them in to Hindley's hand with a slight nod.

Michael's funeral was held at St Francis Monastery with every seat in the church taken, leaving some people to stand. A requiem mass was said and people prayed and said their goodbyes on 21st June 1957.

The Gorton and Openshaw Reporter printed a list of mourners who had attended the funeral. Hindley's name was not on the list and later she declared: "I could not go to his funeral because I was frightened; his death was hard to come to terms with. It made me realise how final death was. He was the first person who had gone from my life for good". The inquest in to Michael's death stated he had drowned after getting a cramp from the cold water; the verdict was one of accidental death.

Day after day she would sit at Michael's grave; she became a Catholic (Michael's Religion) and would go to church with his mother to pray.

For a long time after his death, she would dress as if still in mourning and wore deep eye make-up.

The Catholic Religions stayed as a major part of her life until Brady convinced her otherwise.

# EPISODE 3

"Shut your eyes and see."
—James Joyce

## James Joyce's Life

James Joyce's life and most of his work are extremely important in our book. People may wonder why a book has been written about two of the most infamous child serial killer's—including writing of a famous Irish Novelist, Poet and some of his works. I would like to say the answer is clear and self explanatory but that is not the case. However as stated earlier on with connections we have made we can say we believe that much about James Joyce and his works influenced Ian Brady and later Myra Hindley.

The period of time here is also very important. The 1920's is a time period in which many books were written and which influenced Brady. This is not just about the classics that he states to have used.

I must stress once again that everything written is based on theory. You will soon begin to notice how many coincidences we have. Just how many coincidences does it take to make one big truth?

The books in general made Erica and the group look at the case differently.

She had noticed the books were being mentioned in everything you read about the Moors Murders. Books in suitcases, books on shelves and visits to libraries especially Chethams Library in Manchester.

Many of the books found at Hattersley are what were classed as "hard to get books"; all had been banned at one time or another in many countries—Ulysses being one of these books.

Reading is what Ian Brady did; everything from poetry to philosophy, politics to history.

We believe Ulysses and Finnegan's wake are extremely important to Brady and Hindley, the crimes they committed and how they lived their lives during the period known as the Moors Murders. More will be explained as the book progresses.

Background on James Joyce's life and the works of Ulysses and Finnegan's Wake are necessary for you to understand our book.

Ulysses is noted for its realism. It is classed as the most realistic book—meaning when you read the book it describes everything that is taking place. This includes the sound of water running to the feelings described first person by the characters.

*Erica Gregory*

James Joyce's work is very complex to read. Finnegan's Wake is full of riddles and crypts and has many layers. It's almost like peeling away an onion, trying to get to the bottom of the genuine meaning. Again this is felt about Brady's complex plans which are full of the same ideas. James Joyce wrote his work in complex notebooks similar to Ian Brady. James Joyce also used things he was influenced by: an example being history—this included Napoleon and Oliver Cromwell. He also used poetry from Wordsworth, Percy Shelley, William Blake, and Shakespeare's plays, Dante and The Greek Myths and Mythology. He mapped his books to areas where he lived. He also included his political views of food and famine, and Religion. He believed that life was an Art.

He included all in his writings. Ulysses, apart from being a love story is also classed as a murder story. As we will show, Ian Brady also included much of what Joyce did, into his plans. So much so he even got Myra to act this period of time out, bringing to life his work.

James Joyce was born in Ireland in 1882. He lived to the age of 59. He grew up to be one of Ireland's best known novelists and poets. James Joyce is best known for his novel Ulysses published in 1922 by Sylvia Beach at the Shakespeare and co bookshop in Paris. Other major works are the collection of short stories known as Dubliners published in 1914. In 1916 there was a novel named "A Portrait of an Artist as a Young Man". James Joyce's final piece of work was 'Finnegan's Wake' in 1939. Other pieces of his work include: 3 books of poetry, a play and occasional journalism. His published letters are now on display.

James Joyce was born into a middle class family in Dublin. Joyce became an outstanding student at every stage during education. He studied at Jesuit schools Clongowes and Belvedere—going on to study at a university in Dublin. When Joyce reached his early twenties he emigrated permanently to continental Europe. He lived in many places including Trieste, Paris and Zurich. Although most of his adult life was spent away from Ireland living abroad, his fictional universe has never strayed far away from Dublin. His characters are also close to home as most of them resemble those of family members, friends and enemies from his time living in Dublin. Joyce once stated: "For myself, I always write about Dublin—because if I can get to the heart of Dublin I can get to the heart of all the cities of the world. In the particular is contained the universe".

The works of James Joyce:

Chamber's music poems 1907

Dubliner's collection of short stories 1914

A portrait of an artist as a young man novel 1916

Exiles play 1918

Ulysses novel 1922

Pomes Penyeach Poems 1927

Collected poems poems 1936

Finnegan's Wake novel 1939

Stephen hero precursor to a 1944

*Erica Gregory*

Portrait written

    Giacomo Joyce 1968

    Letters of James Joyce vol.1 1968

    The critical writings of James Joyce 1959

    The Cat and the Devil—published 1968

    Letters of James Joyce vol 2—published 1966

    Letters of James Joyce vol 3—published 1966

    Selected letters of James Joyce—published 1975

    The cats of Copenhagen—published 2012

# EPISODE 4

> "I've put in so many enigmas and puzzles that it will keep the professors busy for centuries
> *James Joyce*

# James Joyce's work:

---

What we would add here is that you give this section a go. The Characters are the most important to read about. The work of Joyce is hard to understand, even for University students. What we are showing here is Brady's intelligence, the reason why no one has figured him out.

Ulysses is a novel by the Irish author James Joyce, it was first serialised in parts in the American journal. The little review (Greenwich Village USA), from March 1918-December 1920, and then published in its entirety by Sylvia Beach in February 1922. In Paris, one of the most important works of modernist's literature, it has been called "a demonstration and summation of the entire movement". "Before Joyce, no writer of fiction had so foregoing the process of thinking". The Bookshop owned by Sylvia Beach, was one where many Artists and writers would go to read books of the type Ian Brady had in the suitcases and on the bookshelves. Banned books and hard to find literature.

*Erica Gregory*

Ulysses chronicles the passage of Leopold Bloom through during an ordinary day, 16th June 1904 {the day of Joyce's first date with his future wife, Nora Barnacle}. Ulysses is the Latin used name of Odyssey, and the novel establishes a series of parallels between its characters and event's and those of the poem {e.g. the correspondence of Leopold Bloom to Odysseys, Molly Bloom to Penelope and Stephen Dedalus to Telemachus}. Joyce fans worldwide now celebrate the June 16$^{th}$ as Blooms day.

Ulysses is approximately 265.000 words in length, uses a lexicon of 30,030 words {including proper names, plurals and various verb tenses}, and is divided into eighteen episodes. Since publication, the book has attracted controversy and scrutiny, ranging from early obscenity trials to protracted textual "Joyce wars ". Ulysses stream-of-consciousness technique, careful structuring and experimental prose-full of puns, parodies and allusions, as well as its rich characterisations and broad humour, made the book a highly regarded novel in the modernist pantheon. In 1998, the modern library ranked Ulysses first on its list of the 100 best English language novels of the 20th century.

Joyce first encountered Odysseus in Charles Lamb's adventures of Ulysses—an adaptation of the odyssey for children, which seemed to establish the Roman name in Joyce's mind. At school he wrote an essay on Ulysses entitled "my favourite hero". Joyce told Frank Budgen that he considered Ulysses the only all-round character in literature. He thought about calling his book Dubliners by the name Ulysses in Dublin, but the idea grew from a story in Dubliners in 1906, to a "short book" in 1907, to the vast novel it became Ulysses. Joyce began writing Ulysses in 1914.

Joyce initially prepared Ulysses in 1902, while Joyce was still only twenty years old. He was self possessed enough to gather all his epiphanies and began arranging them to form notes for Ulysses. He began work in earnest in 1914, after the publication of a Portrait of an artist as a young man, and it was eventually published in 1922.

Ulysses deals with opulence of personal thought and while we are ushered into its characters private worlds with ease, we know little about exteriors. The narrative parallels Homer's Odyssey, but on in depth knowledge of the odyssey is not necessary for enjoyment of Ulysses.

The main character in the book is Leopold Bloom, a non-practising Jew. Throughout the novel the reader is permitted to become wholly familiar with the inner workings of Leopold's mind, but not given enough information about the physical appearance to form a clear mental picture of him. We are told that he is quiet and decent, a man of inflexible honour to his fingertips. He has a pale intellectual face in which are set two dark large lidded, superbly expressive eyes.

The story of a haunting sorrow is written on his face and his friends say that there's a touch of the artist about old Bloom: a safe, moustached man who has his good points and slips off when the fun gets too hot.

Another significant figure winding his way through the streets of Dublin in Ulysses is Stephen Dedalus, whom we first meet in A Portrait of an Artist as a Young Man. Stephen is arrogant young intellectual whom Bloom takes under his wings. He acts like a father figure to the young Stephen who fulfils the role to some extent of a son for Bloom, whose own son died in infancy.

Molly Bloom in Ulysses is equated with Penelope in the Odyssey and the last chapter of the book id dedicated solely to her meanderings and musings. It is one of the renowned pieces of writing in Ulysses and is famous for its celebration of this voluptuous, sensuous, opulent, abundant, independent, lush and blooming woman.

Some of the main characters in Ulysses are significant to the working out we have for Brady and Hindley's actions. Firstly I will supply a background of the significant characters in the book and later you will get to understand the links we have or coincidences as some people may like to call them.

Leopold Bloom functions as a sort of everyman a bourgeois Odysseus for the twentieth century. At the same time, the novels depiction of his personality is one of the most detailed in all literature. Bloom is a thirty eight year old advertising canvasser. His father was a Hungarian Jew, and Joyce exploits the irony of this fact that Dublin's latter-day Odysseus is really a Jew with Hungarian origins—to such an extent that readers often forget Blooms Irish mother and multiple baptisms. Blooms status as an outsider, combined with his own ability to envision an inclusive state, make him a figure that both suffers from and exposes the insularity of Ireland in 1904. Yet the social exclusion of Bloom is not a simple one-sided.

Bloom is clear-sighted and mostly unsentimental when it comes to his male peers. He does not like to drink often or to gossip, and though he is always friendly, he is not sorry to be excluded from their circles.

When Bloom first appears in episode four of Ulysses, his character is noteworthy for its differences from Stephen's character, on which the first three episodes focus. Stephen's celibacy makes Bloom comfort with the physical world seem more remarkable. This ease accords with his practical mind and scientific curiosity. Whereas Stephen, in episode three, shuts himself off from material world to ponder the workings of his own perception, Bloom appears in the beginning of episode four bending down to his cat, wondering how senses work. Bloom's comfort with the physical also manifests itself in his sexuality, a dimension mostly absent from Stephen's character. We get ample evidence of Bloom's sexuality—from his penchant for voyeurism and female understanding to his masturbation and erotic correspondence while Stephen seems inexperienced and celebrate. Other disparities between the two men further define Bloom's character; where Stephen is depressive and somewhat dramatic, Bloom is mature and even headed. Bloom possesses the ability to cheer himself up and to pragmatically refuse to think about depressing topics. Yet Bloom and Stephen are similar too. They are both un-realised artists. If with complexly different agendas, as one Dubliner puts it, "we might say that Bloom's conception of art is bourgeois, in the sense that he considers art as a way to affect people's actions and feelings in an immediate way. From his desire to create a newer; better advertisement, to his love poem for Molly, to his reading of Shakespeare for its moral value, Bloom's version of art does not stray far from real-life situations. Blooms sense of culture and his aspiration to be "cultured" also seems to bring him close to Stephen. The two men share a love for music and Stephen's companionship is attractive to Bloom, who would love to be an expert, rather than a dabbler, in various subjects.

Two emotional crises plagues Bloom's otherwise cheerful demeanour throughout Ulysses—the breakdown of his male family line and the infidelity of his wife, Molly. The untimely deaths of both Blooms Father {by Suicide} and his only son, Rudy {days after his birth} leads Bloom to feel cosmetically lonely and powerless. Bloom is allowed a brief respite from these emotions during his union with Stephen in the latter part of the novel. We slowly realise over the course of Ulysses that the first crisis of the family line is related to the second crisis of the marital infidelity; the Bloom's intimacy and attempts at the procreation have broken down since the death of their son eleven years ago. Bloom's reaction to Molly's decision to look elsewhere {to Blazes Boylan} for sex is complex. Bloom enjoys the fact that other men appreciate his wife, and he is generally a passive, accepting person. Bloom is clear sighted enough to realise, though, that Blazes Boyle is a paltry replacement for himself, and he ultimately cheers himself by recon text valuing the problem. Boylan is only one of many, and it is Molly that Bloom should concentrate his own energies.

In fact, it is this ability to shift perspective by sympathising with another viewpoint that renders Bloom heroic. His compassion is evident through-out he is charitable to animals and people in need, his sympathies extend even to a woman in labour. Blooms masculinity is frequently called into question by other characters; hence, the second irony of Ulysses is that Bloom as everyman is also somewhat feminine and it is precisely his fluid, androgynous capacity to empathise with people and things of all types and to be both a symbolic father and mother to Stephen that makes him the hero of the novel.

There is a timeline below showing an idea of the book. How the day is mapped out at paces around Dublin and times of day. This book is even hard for well read students and teachers to understand, just so you can see how complex the research has been for the group.

## Episode four Calypso

* First we encounter Bloom at 8am at his house at 7 Eccles Street making breakfast for his wife, Molly.

* Bloom feeds their cat and thinks about how the world looks from the cat's point of view. He realises he has to go to the butcher's to get food for his wife.

* Bloom head's out to the butcher's, leaving the door open a crack since he doesn't have his latchkey. He daydream's on his way there. He stops at the grocer's and makes small talk about Dignam{ a mutual friend who died and whose funeral is today}.

* At the butcher's, Bloom finds himself in line behind his neighbour's daughter. He can't help himself and ogles her.

* Walking out, an advertisement for a Zionist colony catches his eye and he considers { not very seriously}buying land from them. Bloom thinks about the Jews history of persecution.

* Bloom thinks of Molly and Milly. A moment of darkness as the sun covers the cloud makes him feel gloomy.

* Returning home, Bloom finds a letter from Milly. There is also a suspicious looking letter from his wife.

* Bloom finishes breakfast and takes it up to Molly, who is still in bed. They discuss a book she is reading, she mocks him for using fancy words when he tries to explain the idea "metempsychosis".

* Bloom realises his kidney is burning {the food he was preparing for breakfast} and rushes down to get it. Downstairs, he reads his letter from his daughter. As he does, he remembers his daughter as a young girl and thinks of his son, Rudy, who died as an infant.

* Bloom thinks of Molly and what she is going to do later that day {first allusion we have to her affair with Boylan}.

* He takes a penny-weekly {local newspaper} to the outhouse out back and reads a prize story while he goes to the bathroom.

# Episode 5 Lotus Eaters

* Its 10am Bloom is about a mile and a quarter from his home on Eccles Street, he's walking to the post office.

* As Bloom walks, he observes people in the street and thinks about the Dead sea.

* At the post office, he puts in his card and opens a letter from Martha Clifford { we learn Bloom is having an illicit correspondence with the pen name Henry Flower}.

* A man names McCoy engages Bloom in conversation about Dignam, whose funeral is today, and about their wives. Bloom tries to pay attention, but eyes women's skirts as they walk by.

* Bloom thinks of his father's suicide. He reaches a hopscotch court and playfully tiptoes thought it.

* Martha Clifford's letter is playful and asks to meet. Bloom knows he will not meet her but already thinks about writing back to her.

* At all Hallows church, Bloom slips in the back door and sits in on the service for a few moments. He thinks about how strange the Catholic service is {remember that Bloom is Jewish} and cuts out before they collect the money offerings.

- Bloom picks up soap for Molly at the chemist, and has an encounter, with a man named Bantam-Lyons in the street. He accidentally gives Lyons a tip on the horse race.

- As Bloom passes the public baths, he thinks ahead to his bath and imagines "the dark tangled curls of his bush floating, floating hair of the stream around the limp father of thousands, a languid floating flower".

# Episode 6 Hades

- At 11am Bloom climbs into a carriage with Martin Cunningham, Mr Powers, and Simon Dedalus {Stephen's father}. They are part of Dignam's funeral procession and gradually make their way to Prospect Cemetery.

- In the carriage, Bloom thinks about the day of Rudy's conception

- When the men salute Blazes Boylan from the carriage, Bloom thinks that he is the "Worst man in Dublin".

- The men heckle a Jewish moneylender, and it is uncomfortable for Bloom. He tells a story about a man who tried to commit suicide, but was saved. The men turn it into a joke.

* Another funeral procession makes Bloom think of Rudy again. Mr Power makes a crack about how disgraceful suicide is. Since Bloom's father committed suicide, he is again made uncomfortable.

* Bloom let's his mind wander, he thinks about Dignam's body and whether or not it could get snagged on a nail.

* The men hop out of the carriage at the ceremony. Bloom is left behind the group, and in his mind, he sympathizes with Dignam's wife.

* Bloom's mind wander's throughout the funeral, he thinks the priest has a swollen face; he wonders why they don't bury people upright; he think's that burying people is a waste of wood.

* Walking out of the cemetery. Bloom points out to John Henry Menton that he has a dent in his hat, Menton snubs him.

# Episode 7 Aeolus

* At noon Bloom goes to the newspaper office of the Freeman Journal to try to secure an ad for a tea, wine and spirit merchant named Keyes.

* He tries to catch the chief editor's attention, but Nannetti hardly gives him the time of day.

* Bloom's mind wanders about in the newspaper office; he imagines falling in to the press and having the newspaper print all over himself and wonders what they do with all the paper after it's not news.

* Bloom looks in on the other men discussing a speech, and he makes small talk with the lawyer J.J O'Molloy.

* Bloom tries to call Keyes about the ad, but misses him. He hears that he is across the street and goes to meet him.

* The newspaper boys go behind him and imitate his walk. While he is gone, the men make fun of Bloom.

* Bloom tries to get another editor's attention as he comes back. Though he secures the ad, the editor is very rude to him.

# Episode 8 Lestrygonians

* At 1pm he is making his way to Davy Byrne's pub.

* Bloom examines a throwaway {Christian paper} that asks him if he was washed in the blood of the lamb.

* He sees one of the Dedalus daughters and thinks about how the house has fallen apart since May Dedalus died.

* At a bridge, Bloom feeds the seagulls. He is offended that they make no sign of thanks.

* Bloom's mind wanders; he thinks about good places for ads, meaning of the word "parallax" {difference in how an object appears seen from two different points of view.} of Molly's rude wit.

* Bloom thinks of his wife, how good she looks when she gets dressed up, and what trouble she puts herself through to look pretty.

* Bloom runs into his old girlfriend, Josie Breen. They discuss her husband and how he is slipping into madness.

* Bloom thinks of his illicit correspondence as he passes the Irish Times office. He thinks about the pains women go though in childbirth.

* A cloud moves over the sun, and Bloom's mood becomes dark and cynical.

* Bloom sees the brother of Charles Stewart Parnell, John Howard and a moment later hears George Russell talking with a young disciple.

* Looking up at the sun, Bloom thinks of astronomy. He remembers walking under the

moon with Molly and Boylan and wonders if they were touching.

* Bloom thinks of how he could never enjoy sex with Molly after Rudy died. He feels his stomach grumble.

* Bloom goes to Burton's restaurant, but is disgusted by the men eating like pigs at a trough. He continues onto Davy Byrne's pub.

* Bloom eats a sandwich and makes awkward small talk with men at the bar.

* Watching two flies stuck in the windowpane, Bloom thinks back to the time he proposed to Molly at Howth's Head. He thinks of the contrast between himself then and himself now.

* Bloom wonders if the statues at the National Library have private parts beneath their skirts. He leaves the bar to pee.

* The men gossip about Bloom, but Byrne sticks up for him and says he seems like a decent guy.

* Bloom pays and leaves the restaurant. His thoughts keep drifting back to Molly, but he tries to e-direct them. He helps a blind old man across the street. He imagines what it must be like to be blind.

* Bloom sees Boylan and panics; he ducks into the library to avoid him.

## Episode 9 Scylla and Charybdis

* While Stephen is explaining his Hamlet theory in the National Library, the head librarian, Lyster, hears that Bloom is looking for old copies of Kilkenny People.

* Later, when Mulligan enters, he reports that he thinks Bloom is gay. He says that he saw him looking up the skirts of the statue of Aphrodite in the lounge.

* When Mulligan and Stephen pass out of the library, Mulligan kids Stephen that Bloom has his eye on him and he must be careful.

## Episode 10: The Wandering Rocks

* We hear a bit of gossip about Bloom from other characters. Lenehan and McCoy joke about how Bloom read a book on astronomy. Lenehan claims that he once groped Molly in a carriage while Bloom sat just across looking out at the stars. McCoy sticks up for Bloom and thinks he has an artistic side.

* While Martin Cunningham takes up his collection for Patrick Dignam, we learn that Bloom quickly

donated five shillings. The other men joke about this.

* Meanwhile, Bloom is at a book cart in Merchant's arch. He reads an erotic passage from Sweets Of Sin and imagines Molly as the female character lusting after him. He buys the book for her, and the owner comments that he has picked a good one.

# Episode 11 Sirens

* Bloom is wandering the streets near the Ormond Hotel. He considers buying paper to write to Martha Clifford.

* Bloom sees Boylan for the third time today and follows him to the bar at the Ormond.

* As Bloom approaches the bar, he runs into Richie Goulding and they agree to have lunch.

* When Boylan leaves, Bloom let out a "light sob of breath" because he knows that he is going to sleep with Molly.

* Goulding talks too much during lunch, and Bloom thinks critically of his verbosity and sympathetically of his chronic back pain.

* The singing in the bar makes Bloom think of Molly and the first time they met playing musical chairs.

* Bloom takes out paper and a pen and begins composing his letter to Martha Clifford.

* Bloom admires the barmaids and feels lonely as the music comes to an end.

* When he goes outside, he sees a prostitute, Birdie Kelley, that he once had an appointment with, He avoids her and let out a big fart as he thinks of Robert Emmet, hero of the song "the croppy boy".

# Episode 12 Cyclops

* A bit after 5pm, Bloom goes to Barney Kiernan's pub hoping to meet Martain Cunningham. He doesn't fit in well with the other men there because he doesn't order a drink.

* The citizen is going on about Irish Nationalism, and when Bloom disagrees with him, they get into an argument. The narrator of the chapter seems to side with the citizen, and makes disparaging comments about Bloom.

* Bloom complains about the persecution of the Jewish people. Then he says "force, hatred, history, all that. That's not life for men and women, insult and hatred. And everybody knows that it's very

opposite of that, which is really life". Alf asks what he is referring to, and he says, "love".

* Bloom leaves for a few moments to look for Martain Cunningham. The men make fun of him viciously, and Cunningham arrives while he is gone.

* The citizen directly attacks Bloom's Jewishness, and Bloom shouts that Christ was a Jew. The citizen is furious and hurls a tin at Bloom as Cunningham's carriage pulls away, but it falls short.

# Episode 13 Nausicaa

* It is 8pm, and the action has moved to the rocks down on Sandy mount Strand where Stephen paused in his morning walk in episode 3.

* For the first half of the episode, a narrator describes the whole scene in extremely sentimental prose, in the style of a romantic girl's novel.

* Bloom eyes the young girl Gerty MacDowell and masturbates behind a rock. Gerty notices the man and in some ways she encourages him.

* Another girl, Cissy, Sees Bloom and goes to ask for the time. He is flustered.

*The Secret Key To The Moors Murders*

* As some fireworks go up out over the bay, Bloom has an orgasm. He feels ashamed of what he has done and begins tidying up. When Gerty stands up, he realizes that she is lame in one foot.

* Bloom thinks about the women he has known in his life, and how incredibly perceptive they all are.

* Noticing that his watch has stopped, Bloom wonders if Molly and Boylan have already slept together.

* Bloom begins to write something in the stand, but then gives up. He takes a short nap on the strand.

# Episode 14 Oxen Of The Sun

* The episode opens at 10pm in the National Maternity Hospital, 29-31 Holles Street, presided over by Sir Andrew Horne.

* Bloom comes into the hospital to wait with the other men there for news of Mina Purefoy giving birth.

* The men are drunk and in very high spirits, Bloom thinks it is inappropriate considering the paining Mrs Purefoy if going through, but he is alone in his opinion.

* Bloom becomes gloomy. When the men leave, he stops it have a word with Nurse Callan, asking her to pass on a kind word to Mina.

* Bloom follows the men to a bar and when Stephen leaves to head to Night town, Bloom follows behind.

# Episode 15, Circe

* The episode opens at midnight by the entrance to Night town, the Dublin red light district. Recall that the episode is written in the form of a play dialogue, and much of it takes place in the form of dreamscapes.

* Bloom follows Stephen and Lynch into Night town. He buy's a pig's cru been and a cold sheep's trotter at a butcher's that is open late.

* Bloom imagines his parents coming back from the dead to scold him for being a failure. Molly appears and also mocks Bloom.

* Josie Breen appears and flirts with Bloom.

* Bloom wonders why he is following Stephen in the first place.

Going back to the Shakespeare and co bookshop and explaining that at the time of the 1920s, Paris was where many famous writers and Artists went to live and study.

We found that Henry Miller, Salvador Dali, Ezra pound, Ernest Hemmingway amongst many others, were mixing together in the area. The life of the Bohemian Artist was very attractive in this period. Living in studios and paying rent from the work they did. A free love period, where you would feel able to experiment and not be condemned as you would be in the UK.

This period of time also brought in the Art of Surrealism and the symbolist movement. Many Artists like Dali, used this in their work. The Art of Surrealism allows the Artist to depict his work in the most graphic way: including death. Symbolists add to their Art, items that stand out, or look out of place in the environment the Art is put. An example of this is a let's say, a purple towel in a black and white bathroom.

I have had to add this as the 1920s has been taken literally in Brady's Art and photography.

Ulysses Characters.

The realities of love and marriage are a prevalent theme in James Joyce's Ulysses and Dubliners, as he attempts to depict the dynamics of the modern relationship and the hardships that develop throughout this cycle. In both texts, Joyce strives to provide a female perspective of marriage that is often lacking in the male-dominated Ireland. Marriage in these texts becomes a struggle between opposing forces: love, regret, and superficiality. Ulysses concludes with Molly Blooms internal monologue, in which the text quite literally follows her complex thought process and the conflicting emotions that she feels towards her husband, Leopold Bloom. Molly examines the many relationships in her life, weighing her past lovers as well as her current suitors with her strange relationship with Leopold. In relation to Penelope, her counterpart from Homers Odyssey, Molly represents a female character grounded in reality that diverges from the idealised image of the innocent and faithful wife that Penelope embodies. The contrast between Molly and Penelope provides a more realistic approach to the typical epic, while simultaneously maintaining some of the qualities that readers are familiar with. Likewise, The Boarding House juxtaposes these opposing notions of marriage through Mrs Mooney and her daughter, Polly. Mrs Mooney's failed marriage is projected onto her expectations for Polly; similarly, the disapproval of the priest provokes Mr Doran to reconsider the idea of marriage to a woman with a lower status than himself. To the characters in The Boarding House, ones image in society becomes more important than love and desire. Regret and the superficial drive the thoughts of the characters in both narratives to the point where love seems like an impossibility. The notion of love is threatened in both of these texts by an anxiety brought about by the superficiality of the modern world.

These characters struggles manifest themselves in the form of internal battles, which reveal an additional layer of unspoken dialogue that exemplifies the complexity of upholding a meaningful relationship in modern society.

From the very first sentence of Penelope, which begins in the middle of a thought, the reader is exposed to the most intimate aspect of a human being: their inner voice. Joyce allows Molly Blooms mind to ponder various recollections that frequently pertain to or lead to the thought of sex, which establishes her as a free woman, as well as primary female voice in Ulysses. Viewing Ulysses as the epic that symbolises Dublin society as a whole, this final chapter is representative of the unheard female voice. Joyce's establishment of Molly as a sexual being both adds to the realism of the narrative as a whole, while simultaneously creating an unconventional female role that defies the boundaries put in place by a society controlled largely by men.

Molly represents the modernist counterpart of Penelope, Odysseus wife in Homers Odyssey. The events that occur throughout the day in Ulysses correlate with those in Odyssey, yet one crucial difference is the depiction of Molly as an unfaithful wife. Penelope, who refuses to give up on her husband's return, remains faithful to Odysseus and does not surrender to the coercion of her many suitors.

She embodies the archetype of the innocent, faithful wife, the polar opposite of Molly Bloom. The paradox of Molly is rooted in the fact that she represents the archetypal figure of Penelope by assuming qualities that directly oppose this very figure. As a modernist interpretation of the Greek epic, Joyce strives to ground the characters in reality, making them flawed and thus relatable as human beings. However, Joyce also references a more traditional love narrative in Molly and Leopold's turbulent, but ultimately hopeful relationship. This combination creates a sense of familiarity while also providing a new angle of the epic for a modern-day audience. In addition, allowing unrestricted access to Molly's innermost thoughts, coupled with the idea of a flawed and relatable human, incites sympathy for the character despite her infidelity. Joyce strays from the notion of the idealises in constructing the thoughts and actions of Molly Bloom, as perfection is an unattainable quality in the realistic depiction of Dublin.

As a stream-of-consciousness narrative, the thoughts swirling in Molly's head during the Penelope chapter naturally jump from one topic to another. Throughout the chapter, her mind is constantly moving between her husband and the various suitors throughout her life, specifically the most recent, Blazes Boylan. The distinction between Leopold and these other men is that Molly focuses on the emotional aspect of her relationship with her husband, while thoughts concerning these other men are somewhat shallow. When her mindwanders to the infidelity with Boylan that took place that same day, her entire focus is on the sexual aspect of their relationship. This relationship is empty in terms of emotion, and Molly is therefore engaging with the superficial aspect of the Dublin lifestyle. In the first paragraph of Penelope, Molly reminisces on her sexual encounter with Boylan earlier that same day, while simultaneously pondering Leopold's past encounters with other women (608-613). Her mind becomes caught up in the emotionless physicality of relationships between human beings, which characterises the superficial nature of relationships in modern times.

These superficial thoughts eventually lead Molly to doubt the strength of her marriage, thus bringing a sense of regret into the text. This regret is indicated in statements such as I could have been a prima Donna but I married

[Leopold] (628). In this chapter, regret is a direct result of superficiality in Dublin, as characters momentarily overlook the meaningful parts of their relationships with one another.

Molly engages with this superficiality through her complex thought process, which leads to the anxiety that her life may have been better had she not married Leopold. Anxiety characterises the emotional crippling brought about by superficiality in the modern world. More specifically, superficiality triggers Molly to reminisce on her unchangeable past decisions rather than focus on the aspects of her life that she actually has control of in the present, thus placing her relationship with Leopold in danger of falling to the emptiness of modern society.

In contrast to the majority of the chapter, the conclusion of Penelope instils a sense of hope for the future of Molly and Leopold, indicating that their relationship is strong enough to withstand this superficiality of modern times. The final word in the narrative, a simple yes, is a powerful confirmation that Molly's emotional connection with Bloom has been meaningful in the past and will continue to be in the future (644). The most interesting aspect of this confirmation is that despite the physical and mental infidelities that both Molly and Leopold have committed throughout this single day, the narrative still ends without a single doubt regarding the integrity and permanence of their marriage. Strangely, both of these characters interact with the superficial during their day, but are constantly being brought back to one another through the various memories and spontaneous thoughts that occur in stream-of-consciousness writing.

The key to understanding the dynamics of Molly and Leopold's resilient marriage lies in the fact that their sexual escapades with other people are often balanced out by an emotional response that triggers the thought of one another. Molly and Leopold therefore perfectly complement each other's personalities in that they both assume characteristics of the opposite sex, thus embodying the idea of an androgynous male and female. Upon re-examining Penelope with this concept, the conflicting nature of Molly's mind, with concern for both the physical aspect of her affair with Boylan as well as her emotional bond with Bloom, is characteristic of both a traditionally male and female thought process. Molly's thoughts reveal a more sexually aggressive and uninhibited side to her that is only seen during this exploration of her inner voice. These thoughts, along with the fact that Molly does act on some of these sexual desires, represents her an envy for men [for] their freedom in sexual matters as well as her subsequent reluctance to accept herself as only a woman (Sadowski 156). This reluctance drives her to view men similarly to the way view women; for example, when reminiscing on her encounter with Boylan earlier that day, she specifically focuses on the fact that he is well endowed. Molly essentially objectifies men and turns the traditional notion of gender roles and privileges on its head. The nature of Molly's character is that she is incapable of identifying with a single gender; on one hand, she fulfils both motherly and spousal obligations, yet on the other, she exudes a more aggressive and masculine confidence through her thoughts and actions. Her affair with Boylan is a prime example of this dichotomy, as she is able to drop everything and act with spontaneity and a self-proclaimed freedom, but she ultimately returns to her womanly obligations at the end of the narrative.

Leopold, who experiences sexual pleasure through women other than Molly throughout the day, possesses some of the typical male characteristics that Molly takes on, but as an androgynous character, he also exhibits many feminine characteristics. At one hallucinatory point in the narrative, these characteristics manifest themselves and literally transform Leopold into a woman, causing him to give birth and receive abuse from Bella at the brothel. This transformation forces Leopold takes into the role of the submissive female, creating an interesting sub-narrative of gender transformation throughout Ulysses. This submissiveness during the hallucination is a direct reference to Leopold's figurative femininity throughout the rest of the text. As the feminine counterpart to Molly's masculinity, Leopold becomes obsessed by Molly and Boylans sexual encounter, which he anticipates for most of his day. Molly places Leopold in a situation where he must submit to his wife's masculine aggressiveness and freedom. However, it is in this alternating relationship that their marriage finds the perfect balance and allows them to maintain their sense of stability.

The psychology of Ulysses presents the complex thought processes of both Molly and Leopold during a single day in Dublin. For the majority of the narrative, it seems as if their marriage will eventually fail due to infidelities on both of their parts. However, Joyce's exploration of these thoughts reveals one important commonality between their minds. Regardless of the infidelity and thoughts of other men or women, both Molly and Leopold's mind always return to the thought of their relationship, which has the most substance of all the relationships in Ulysses. For example, in Penelope, despite Molly's seeming regret for past decisions, along with thoughts of her past suitors, her mental being ultimately returns to the point in her relationship with Leopold where he proposes to her. In terms of this marriage, the narrative ends with the beginning, which signifies that at the end of this long and eventful day, their relationship has been renewed and is in fact stronger than it has been at any other point in the narrative. The fact that Leopold and Molly are both androgynous creates a perfect balance between the two; where one exhibits more feminine features, the others masculinity complements these features perfectly, and vice-verse.

A complex exploration of gender roles is a highly visible theme throughout Ulysses, which also contributes to this notion of the superficial in modern relationships. As Leopold and Molly demonstrate, genders are not easily definable in Ulysses. Both masculinity and femininity in the text are relatable to this concept of superficiality, as they both prevent the development of a meaningful relationship.

Masculinity causes infidelity while femininity leads to submissiveness, and therefore, entrapment in the characters own minds. The androgynous character reconciles these two extremes, allowing the shortcomings of both to be countered by one another, creating a point of equilibrium.

The masculine and feminine extremes act as Joyce's criticism of gender norms as they appear in daily life in Dublin. Joyce employs the lasting bond between Molly and Leopold to demonstrate that a meaningful relationship in a world full of superficiality is a combination of these two extremes. Joyce suggests that a clear-cut gender system pits one extreme in conflict with another, whereas finding a balance between the two creates meaningful and lasting relationships. Similar to his other works, Joyce places the solution for Molly and Leopold in the idea of balance rather than extremism, which combats and ultimately trumps the superficiality of modern society and the threat it poses to a significant relationship.

Joyce's Dubliners, specifically The Boarding House, depicts a struggle similar to Molly and Leopold's in Ulysses. Mrs Mooney's boarding house, which acts as a symbol for Dublin society as a whole, is the microcosm where the three main characters struggle to form meaningful relationships. Mrs Mooney, her daughter Polly, and Mr Doran all experience a form of anxiety and the pressure of superficiality as it pertains relationships. Many of the same themes regarding a meaningful relationship that appear in Ulysses are also apparent in The Boarding House. Mrs Mooney's past infringes on the present, causing her to stress the importance of status rather than true love to Polly. Similarly, Mr Doran is enslaved by the proper image that one must uphold in a superficial society, causing him to doubt his love for Polly. Joyce again focuses on the psychological aspect of these characters to create realistic internal struggles that produces a sense of regret and initiates a paralysis that hinders the situations progress.

Mrs Mooneys past experiences, as well as the woman she has become, is reminiscent of the psychologically complex Molly Bloom. At the beginning of the novel, the first thing that is revealed about Mrs Mooney is that her former husband was a drunk who went for [her] with the cleaver, thus causing them to separate (38). Similar to Molly Bloom, whose thoughts begin to focus on the past, Mrs Mooney's past haunts her in the present, which forms her attitude toward the notion of her daughter Polly getting married. Mrs Mooney turns the process of relationships and marriage into a business, where she silent monitors and judgers her daughters suitors. The narrative refers to her judgement of the men in the boarding house who flirt with Polly. The narrator states that Mrs Mooney knew that the young man were only passing the time away; none of them meant business (39). The reference to the process of winning over her daughters affection as a business indicates that Mrs Mooney has been conditioned to act as though real feelings are not a part of this process. Her past marriage to her abusive husband has caused her to approach relationships in a business—like sense and suppress emotions as a defence mechanism against the possibility of her daughter ending up in a dangerous situation like she was once in. Like Molly Bloom, certain regret for past decisions manipulates Mrs Mooney's reason in the present. In this sense, the past is very much a living entity that influences behaviour and thoughts in the present.

Mrs. Mooney, like Molly Bloom, interacts with the superficiality of the modern world in her treatment of her daughters many suitors. The narrator states that Polly has previously flirted with a disreputable man who would come into her workplace each day; Mrs Mooney responds to this knowledge by taking her daughter home again and [setting] her to do housework (39). This indicates that Mrs Mooney has shifted her concern for her daughters future from true love to status in society.

Similar to the sexual thoughts of Boylan that Molly has, Mrs Mooney's past experience has caused her to lose concern for any relationship with substance and ascribe to the shallowness of modern relationships.

Based on her system of approval for her daughters love interests, marriage is a means by which one profits and moves up the social ladder above all else. Mrs Mooney limits and thus traps her daughter in this system, infringing on her own free will because of the emotional hardening that has occurred within herself and has caused her to align with superficiality.

The notion of androgyny appears in The Boarding House, yet unlike Ulysses, where androgyny brings about a balance to the extremes of femininity and masculinity, it only reinforces the empty relationships between characters in the narrative. According to Earl G. Ingersoll, Mrs Mooney assumes masculinity through her activity and decisiveness, while simultaneously taking on femininity with a concern for detail. Mrs Mooney ultimately decides whom Polly will marry, yet during this process, she carefully scrutinises the relationships that her daughter forms. In this sense, she is both the mother and father figure for her daughter. Though Mrs Mooney does reach a point where her masculine and feminine characteristics balance out, they do so in such a way that it enhances her ability to disconnect from emotions and continue her business of finding a proper suitor for her daughter.

Again, her past experience with her former husband is the main perpetrator in this case, as she has become acclimatized to running every aspect of her life similar to how she operates her boarding house. Mrs Mooney thus becomes the plotter of the narrative, who acts as both one of the obstacles to attaining real love and a character that draws sympathy from the reader. In the Dublin of Ulysses, androgyny and a sense of balance brings about a solution, whereas in The Boarding House, they only perpetuate the superficiality of the business that forming relationships has become.

Polly's encounters with Mr Doran begin to flourish into a relationship, at which point Mrs Mooney begins to quietly scrutinise them. Mr Doran's status and success in life is not an issue, so Mrs Mooney arranges a meeting where she will attempt to coerce him into marrying Polly. At this point, the narrative switches over to Mr Doran's viewpoint, in which it is revealed that he is experiencing anxiety due to the pressures of a society concerned with appearance and status. He, like Mrs Mooney, is affected by the notion of social status; however, he is more concerned with the fact that he will be marrying a woman of lower status, which is worsened by a priests criticism of his affair with Polly during confession. The theme of extremism appears at this point in the narrative, as Mr Doran is placed in a position where he must decide whether he will marry Polly or abandon her completely. These two extremes render Mr Doran helpless. Following his rationale, both extremes will negatively impact his reputation, thus placing a paralysis on his life at this crossroad.

In Mr Doran's case, the superficiality of modern times completely disallows the notion of a relationship based on true love, and instead allows only for a relationship based on class and appearance to the rest of society.

Mr Doran and Mrs Mooney's dilemmas in The Boarding House are a direct reflection of the obstacles that Molly and Leopold overcome throughout the day. Mrs Doran embodies the idea of the balance found in androgyny, while Mr Doran is characterised by the restricting effects of extremism in Dublin society. The boarding house itself, which acts as a miniaturised Dublin in the interactions between characters and in the way it is operated by Mrs Mooney, indicate an on-going struggle of producing meaning in a society that thrives on superficiality. The shortcomings of extremism and the necessity of balance in life are apparent themes throughout the majority of Joyce's texts. Extremisms appearance in both of these narratives, which causes psychological conflict within each of these characters, acts as Joyce's criticism of a black-and-white world where one must align him or herself on one side or the other.

The other common theme in both of these narratives, balance, is the point at which the narratives diverge. In contrast to Ulysses, in which Leopold and Molly ultimately find their sense of balance, The Boarding House, as well as the other stories in Dubliners, lack real solutions to the characters dilemmas. This fact is in line with the open nature of all of the conclusions in Dubliners. These narratives generally end without a solid conclusion and leave the reader guessing what crucial decision the characters will come to. Though there is a degree of uncertainty in both narratives, Ulysses concludes with a sense of hope for the future of Leopold and Mollys marriage. While The Boarding House hints that Mr. Doran will ultimately ask Polly to marry him, the narrative never brings closure to his previous concern about marrying into the lower class, leaving the reader questioning the longevity of their relationship. The only clues the reader is granted are Mr. Dorans paralysis as well as his doubts towards marrying Polly. The fact that Joyce leaves only these details to his readers creates a very negative atmosphere, especially when considered with the lack of conclusion to the story. Very little is certain within Dubliners as a whole, but one common thread that brings the stories together is found in the sudden endings that leave the narrative open on a low point.

Where the future for Molly and Leopold possesses some degree ofcertainty for a long-lasting relationship, the lack of any certainty atthe end of The Boarding House, coupled with Mr.Dorans doubts about Polly, hints that their union will likely fail at some point in the future. Therefore, in The Boarding House, superficiality is never overcome, leaving meaningful relationships to become obsolete in the modern world.

With Ulysses and The Boarding House, Joyce imagines two distinct views of Dublin. Both of these narratives are common in the sense that they explore the dynamics of a relationship in a world characterised by the superficial. Both texts also relate the idea of the androgynous character as it relates to extremism in Dublin. In Ulysses, androgyny functions as a combatant of superficiality, allowing Molly and Leopold to counter the male and female aspects of one another and thus develop into the a couple that interconnects almost perfectly. The imperfect nature of both Molly and Leopold creates characters that the reader can both identify and thus sympathise with. Regardless of her imperfections, Molly acts as the modern-day counterpart to the Odyssey's Penelope, in that at the end of her day, she and her husband have been reunited, and their life together will begin again the next day. Despite her infidelities, Molly is essentially the less-idealised image of Penelope in the midst of a material and superficial society.

Ultimately, both Leopold and Molly's imperfections lead them back to one another and into a hopeful future for their marriage. The Boarding House provides a darker view of the modern relationship in Dublin.

While androgyny is also a prevalent theme in regards to Mrs. Mooney, a concern for the superficial caused by past experiences hinders these characters from making any progress towards a meaningful relationship.

The primary concern with Mrs. Mooney and Mr. Doran continues to be appearance, which continues to define relationships in the microcosm of Dublin that the boarding house represents. The lack of any closure in The Boarding House is the polar opposite of the conclusion of Ulysses, in that the negative tone expresses uncertainty for the future of Mr. Doran and Polly. The characters in The Boarding House represent the full effects of modernity and superficiality on relationships. When compared to Molly and Leopold, the imminent failure of the characters in Dubliners attests to the strength of Molly's marriage.

Despite their shortcomings and interactions with the superficial, Molly and Leopold are still able to maintain a relationship with true love as its foundation. Both narratives demonstrate the hardships of forming and preserving a stable relationship with the many instabilities of a society that allows superficiality to become such a prominent characteristic of interactions between people. The fact that Molly and Leopold ultimately return to one another after their eventful day has come to a close indicates that their love is characterised by both immense strength as well as longevity.

## STEPHEN DEDALUS.

"The artist, like the God of creation, remains within or behind or beyond or above his handiwork, invisible, refined out of existence, indifferent, paring his fingernails. quote Joyce

The character of Stephen Dedalus is a harshly drawn version of Joyce himself at the age of twenty two.

Stephen first appeared as the main character of A Portrait Of An Artist As A Young man, which follows his development from early childhood to his proud and ambitious days before leaving Dublin for Paris and the realisation of his artistic capabilities. When we meet Stephen again at the beginning of Ulysses, it is over two years after the end of A Portrait. Stephen has been back in Dublin for over a year, having returned to sit at his mothers deathbed. Stephens artistic talent is still unrealised he is currently a reluctant teacher of history at a boys school. He is disappointed and moody and is still dressed in mourning over the death of his mother almost a year ago. Stephen's interactions with various characters Buck, Haines and Mr Deasy in the opening episodes of the book crystallise our sense of the damaging ties and obligations that have resulted from Stephens return to Ireland. At the beginning of Ulysses, Stephen is a self-conscious young man whose identity is still in formation. Stephens aloofness and his attempts to understand himself through fictional characters such as Hamlet dramatized his struggle into solidify this identity.

Stephen is depicted as above most of the action of the novel. He exists mainly within his own world of ideas his actions in the world tend to pointedly distance himself from others and from the world itself. His freeness with money is a less demonstration of his generosity than of his lack of material concerns. His unwashed state similarly reflects his removal from the material world.

His cryptic stories and riddles cut others off rather than include them as he stubbornly holds a grudge. Our admiration of his noble struggle for Independence is tempered by our knowledge of the impoverished siblings he had left behind. If Stephen himself is an unsympathetic character, however, the issues central to his identity struggle are easier for us to sympathise with, from his contemplation of the perception of the outside world to his teaching of a history lesson to his meditation on aromatics or "mothers love", Stephens mental meanderings centre on the problem of whether, and how; to be an active or passive being within the world.

Stephens struggle tends to centre around his parents. His mother, who seems to blame Stephen for refusing to pray at her deathbed, represents not only a mothers love but also the church and Ireland.

Stephen is haunted by his mothers memory and ghost in the same way that he is haunted by memories of his early platy. Through Stephen's father is still alive and well, we see Stephen attempting to ignore or deny him throughout all of Ulysses. Stephen's struggle with his father seems to be abouts Stephens need to have space in which to create a space untainted by Simon Dedalus's overly critical judgements.

Stephen's struggle to define his identity without the con-strait or aid imposed by his father bleeds into larger conflicts Stephen's struggle with the authority of god, the authority of the British empire even with the authorise of the mocker joker.

Stephen Dedalus is character who is classed as a Bohemian Artist. He is based on the French poets of the 19th Century. One is Arthur Rimbaud. A poet, who at a tender age of 17 was more like a man double his age. A rebellious character who could scare anyone who met him. Intelligent and of a hard nature. James Joyce included him in his work and based Stephens's character partly on him. Rimbaud, like many poets and artists, engaged in experimental sexual activities. Homosexual and of a sadistic nature. Like Sade, who again if you read about him was the same, these Artists were also revolutionaries. Rimbaud's poetry was a major influence on the surrealist and symbolists in their work. Something also that

Rimbaud was known to do was drink Absinthe. This drink has been used by many to bring creativity into their work. The Green Goddess will be explained, we believe this could be why Ian Brady stated "I have always been drawn to the Green" and something we do know is the Green mist, he said he met and made a pact with.

Stephen Dedalus also had a food phobia, and eventually stopped eating. This is a political symbol which Joyce added to signify the hunger strikes by many prisoners in Ireland. Again why is it that Ian Brady decided that he would go without food? This is a symbol of a cracked identity. You need to realise that he did this after he reported abuse by staff at Ashworth, but also at a time he and Myra seemed to be in a broken relationship.

Millicent {Milly} Bloom. Modelled on Lucia Joyce, daughter to James and Nora Joyce.

"Whatever spark of gift I possess has been transmitted to Lucia" quote James Joyce Millie does not actually appear in Ulysses. except in the thoughts of Leopold and Molly and in the somewhat indiscreet gossip of young Alec Bannon. She is fifteen years old and Molly and Leopold have decided to send her to study photography in Mullingar, where she is living. It's there that she met Bannon,who appears in "Oxen Of The Sun" hoping to buy condoms before he heads back to her.

Since the death of their son Rudy, Milly is the Blooms only surviving child. Leopold dotes on her, and remembers her with great affection in "Calypso". Both Leopold and Molly receive correspondence from Milly,

But Leopold gets a full letter whereas Molly only gets a card. In "Penelope" it becomes clear that there is some level of tension between Molly and Milly. Molly appears Jealous of her daughter's beauty and popularity among young men, and suspects that Leopold only sent her off to Mullingar because he could see the affair with Boylan coming. As we learn throughout Ulysses, we can't really trust any of these perspectives and hence know pretty much nothing of Milly Bloom. Her parents reflections on her are more notable for what they say about Leopold and Molly than they are for what they say about Molly.

## Malachi {Buck} Mulligan

Buck Mulligan is a Dublin medical student, and a companion of Stephen Dedalus. Like Dedalus, he has cast off many of the traditional belief structures and social constraints that might confine a young Irishman's life, but unlike Stephen he is extremely irreverent; he doesn't seem to respect anything.

In this sense, Mulligan functions as something of an alter ego for Stephen. As impossible a character as Dedalus can be to get your head around, its by noting his contrasts with Mulligan that you begin to understand what are Stephen's values. About all perhaps, is self respect. On top of Martello tower, Mulligan tells Stephen that he overheard him call Stephen's mother "beastly dead". Mulligan is briefly embarrassed but quickly begins making excuses and talking himself back into boldness. Stephen carefully explains that it was not so much the offence to his mother that bothered him as the offence to himself.

It's not immediately apparent but as Ulysses goes on, it becomes clear that Mulligan is something of a parasite. He constantly makes jokes at Stephens's expense, but also steals almost all of his ideas from Stephen. After hearing Stephen's Hamlet theory, Mulligan conceives an irrelevant play, everyman his own wife or a honeymoon in the hand, which both plagiarises and mocks Stephen's ideas. As Bloom puts it he's "picking your brains".

Mulligan is witty, clever and extremely well educated, but its clear that he is jealous of Stephen. Perhaps the only reason his jealousy doesn't overtake him is what he tells Haines in the Episode The Wandering Rocks that Stephen will write something of a note in ten years, Mulligan doesn't seem like a character who could imagine devoting himself to anything for ten years and anyway that leaves him nine years to mock.

* They go down the the bay and Buck goes swimming. When Stephen leaves. Buck asks him for the tower key and two pence.

Is this a character given to David Smith maybe?.

## FINNEGANS WAKE

Again a very complex book, but we feel very important as a continuation to stories Brady used in real life. You will see just how complex Joyce's mind was.

Drive westwards out of Dublin, keeping south of Phoenix park, and you will come to Chapelizod. The name means "chapel or iseult", whom this Irish known as Isoilde and the Germans as Isolde—tragic heroine or Wagner's opera. There is little that is romantic about Chapelizod nowadays; if you want minimum excitement you will have to go to the pubs, of which the most interesting is purely fictional the Bristol. Some will identify this for you with the dead man, so called because the customers would roll out drunk and be run over by trams. It is important to us because its landlord is the hero of Finnegan's Wake. He is middle aged, of Scandinavian stock and a protestant upbringing, and he has a wife who seems to have some Russian blood in her. His name is, as far as we can tell, Mr Porter, appropriate for a man who carries up crates of Guinness from the cellar, and he is the father of 3 young children two of which are twin boys called Kevin and Jerry, and he has a pretty little daughter named Isobel.

Mr Porter and his family are asleep for the greater part of the book. It has been a hard Saturday evening in the public bar, and sleep prolongs itself some way into the peace of Sunday morning. Mr Porter dreams hard, and we are permitted to share his dream. In its various preoccupations of his are fantastcated, and the chief of these are complex obsession to be expected in a man aware of ageing; his day is passing and the new age belongs to his sons, particularly his favourite son Kevin; his wife no longer attracts him. He looks for a last sexual fling, or even a renewal of the sexual impulse, in a younger woman. All this is innocent enough and should not give him any bad dreams, but it happens that his desires are fixed on his own daughter. "incest" is a terrible word, even though it means nothing more than a loyal desire to keep sex within the family, and Mr Porters dream will only admit the word in disguise as "insect". Sleeping, he becomes remarkable mixture of guilt man beast, and crawling thing, and he even takes on a new and dreamily appropriate name Humphrey Chimp-den Earwicker. There we have the hump of sexual guilt he carries on his back (he is a different porter now) a hint of the ape, and more than a hint of the insect. "Earwicker" is done to "earwig", and this, through the French Perce-Oreille, can be Hibernicised into "Persse O'Reilly". Another preoccupation is a disire to be accepted by the Irish people, as a leader of a political representative, but he remains aware of the foreignness that his dream name to well indicates, and "Persse O'Reilly" is there only for mockery or execration.

In his dream HCE, as we shall now call him, tries to make the whole of history swallow up his guilt for him. His initials are made to stand for the generality of sinful man, and they are extended into slogans like "here comes everybody" and "haveth childers everywhere". After all, sexual guilt presupposes a certain creative or procreative vitality and a fall only comes to those who are capable of an erection. The unquenchable vitality appears in "our human conger Eel" (despite the "down wantons down" of the eel pie makerin King Lear); the erector of great structures is seen in "Howth Castle and Environs!. From the point of view of the ultimate dreamer of the dream, though (the author himself), to be used to exemplify the doctrine of the cycle. HCE, is in fact a very ordinary innkeeper, but Jouce knows what he is doing. He obligingly falls into a trance himself and dreams a cunning dream which encloses that of his hero, a dream which confers the author's own special knowledge on the unlearned snorer, granting him the gift of tongues (this universal history and hence polyglot) as well as such trifles as the ability to expound the Cabala and the Tunc page of the book of Kells. Ho goes further. When HCE and his wife are awakened by the crying of one of the twins and, when quietening the child, they attempt intercourse, Joyce does all the dreaming himself; the sleeping quality of the book must not be lost, the dream must remain unbroken. The introduction of waking attitudes and waking language would be an intolerable shock to the system and it would be artistic sin to mix two orders of reality.

## (ii)

Even if we abandon the straight line view of history, Starting as Julius Caesar, say and ending with the late President Kennedy, we cannot have a history book, even a dream one, without a large cast of characters. With the authors help HCE must people his sleeping world with a vast number of personages, all of whom must exemplify the fall-rise-fall principle which is made to animate Vico's cycle. At the same time, since this a work of art, certain rules of economy must be observed rules which true history. Which is over-fecund of characters, chooses to ignore. What HCE does in his sleep is to turn his family into a kind of amateur dramatic society which, with help from customers, the cleaning women, the pub handyman and a few others, is prepared to impersonate, however unhandily, a whole corpus of beings from myth and literature (including popular magazines, brainstorming melodramas and doubtful street ballads) as well as from history books. In a dream it is proper for fictional characters and historical personages to occur the one zone of reality, as well as to mix their times and subsist happily together on a kind of supra-temporal level; it is the most natural thing in the dreamer's world to see Dr Johnson and Falstaff, as well as the women next door, waiting on Charing Cross railway station. The only significant date in HCE'S version of history is 1132ad, and the significance is entirely symbolic; 11 stands for the return or return or reinstatement or recovering or resumption (having counted up to 10 on our fingers we have to start again for 11); 32 feet per second is the rate of acceleration of all falling bodies, and the number itself will remind us of the fall of Adam, Humpty Dumpty, Napoleon, Parnell and also of HCE himself, who is all their reincarnations.

A knowledge of this easy symbolism is essential for an understanding of Finnegan's Wake, as it is also the realisation of the importance of number in general. You can build up the supporting dream-cast of the play by abstracting numbers from the calendar that hangs on some wall or other in the Bristol Tavern. There are four weeks in a lunar month, and these will give you the four old men who have so much to say, though what they have to say is rarely of much value—Matthew Gregory, Mark Lyons, Luke Tarpey and Johnny MacDougal. They are the four go-spellers, as well as the four provinces of Ireland, and they take off to impersonal regions where they represent the four points of the compass, the four elements, the four classical ages and so on. They are always together, followed by their donkey, and it is in order to think of them as single units, their names truncated to ha, ma,lu and Jo and crushed together to make Hamalyjo. They end up in the fading of the dream, as four bed posts. There are twelve months in a year, and these will give us the twelve Sullivan's or Doyle's customer's in HCE'S bar but also twelve apostles and twelve jurymen always ready to give ounderous judgement in polysyllables ending in "ation". Their number as with a jury is more important than their names, which are always changing; when we meet a catalogue of apparently new characters, it is enough for us ti take a breath and count. We shall usually find the same old twelve. The month of February (in which James Joyce was born) has sometimes 28 days, sometimes twenty nine. This provides Joyce with a bevy of girls from the academy of St Bride's (St Bridget's or Ireland herself) with a separable special girl who usually turns out to be Isobel. HCE'S own daughter, divide 28 by 4 and you are left with 7. The month maidens sometimes form themselves into the seven colours of the rainbow an important emblem in Finnegan's Wake. Since it signifies god's covenant after the flood hope of reinstatement after sin eleven after thirty two.

One of the interesting things about Finnegans Wake is the way in which number refuses to melt and become fantasticated. This dream differs then from our own dreams, in which we take two slices of cake from a plate holding twelve and finding only seven left. When HCE'S dream wife gives gifts to each of her one hundred and eleven children, there are (i have counted) exactly one hundred and eleven, no more no less. When the thunder of man's fall sounds or the thunder of gods wrath, we find this represented by a word of exactly one hundred letters no more no less. One sometimes becomes two but that is a natural process of cellular fission; the father has begotten two sons, and the two sons together make up the parents body. This encourages Joyce to present the one daughter Isobel as two girls a split personality, a temptress in love only with her mirror image. But there is never any woman deformation of a significant number; simple arithmetic is the very breath of this dream.

The four, the twelve and the twenty eight or twenty nine tend to stand outside of history and comment on it. The hard work of the participation in the recurrent story of the man's fall and resurrection rests on the shoulders of HCE, his wife and family and the cleaning woman Kate. The mythical literary and histirical characters who best ememplify the story are chosen out of a fairly narrow field mainly from Irish history. Its mainly from those Irish personages who's sins or fall best bodies firth HCE'S own guilt. In other words, we must expect to meet a man who indulged in, or perhaps merely contemplated acts of illicit love—often with girls for younger than themselves. There must be a tang of incestuous sin. After the general fall motif incarnated in the figures of Adam, Humpty Dumpty we come to particular identifications. HCE plays the parts of Charles Stuwart Parnell, the Irish leader whose love for Kitty O'Shea led to his downfall. A symbol of guiltis taken from the letters which the Irish journalist Piggot forged as part of the general campaign to destroy Parnell. Piggot misspelled "hesitancy" as "hesitancy" and commited the sane solecism when giving evidence before the Parnell commission. This led to his near collapse of his crime. Changes are rung on the misspelling throughout Finnegans Wake and the word its self is especially appropriate to HCE, since his guilt expresses itself in a speech hesitation or stutter. But there is an implication of betrayal and victimisation; a hearsay sin(in the dream HCE crime is no more than that) is swollen into an omnibus accusation which leads to HCE'S trial, incarceration and burial. Parnell who only committed adultery was turned by his enemies into the father of all sin.

Jonathan Swift had an obscure relationship with two girls Esther Johnson and Ester Vanessa. A father in god (swift was of course the dean of St Patrick's in Dublin) evinced a somewhat unfatherly interest in two of his spiritual daughters and these two young women are conjoined in Finnegans Wake in the personality of HCE;S daughter Isobel. Two girls with one Christian name, two girls representing one temptation it is no wonder that the dream Isobel so easily splits herself into two. Here anyway is another guilt pattern from history and like that "hesitancy_hesitancy", it can be alluded ti a single word; Isobels endearment "ppt", and all its allomorphs, come straight from the "little language" or Swifts journal to Stella.

Another legend with strong Irish associations is teased, in this dream out of Isobel's own name. Isobel is Iseult-la-Bella and Chapelizod is her secular shrine. Tristram of Lyonesse came to Ireland to convey Iseult, chosen bride to his uncle King Mark of Cornwall. But Tristram and Iseult fell in love, and a train of subterfuge guilt and disloyalty was started. Both HCE'S preoccupations find potent expression here—aged Mark too old for love, superseded by a younger man, the agonizing sweetness of forbidden realationship. But we can go further Sir Armory Tristram (Tristram of Armorica or Brittany) founded the St Lawrence family of Howth in Dublin and built Howth castle; a dream identification of the two Tristrams is inevitable. For that matter we have two Iseults who, like the two Esthers belong to the one legend King Marks bride and the Iseult of the white hands whom Tristram and Lyonesse eventually married. These are both naturally contained in Isobel and a further justification for the splitting of her identity is provided. We have a verbal leit motif for Parnell and for Swift; we have one for Tristane too, and Joyce likes it from Wagner's version of the legend his music drama Tristan and Isolde. The opening line of Isolde's aria over the body of slain Tristan is "mild and keise" (soft and gentle); this becomes distorted in Finnegans Wake to the grotesque nickname "Mildrew Aisa".

We can find other identifications with Irish legend and history, some of which creep away from the fall-theme and elevate HCE to the role of proud and gutless leader Brian Boru, Finn MacCool, King Laoghair (or Leary). But though the forground of the dream is Dublin, HCE is a universal father figure and we must nopt be surprised if he plays the part of Noah, Julius Ceaser, a Russian general, Harold the Saxon, a Norwegian captain and so on. Scandinavian roles, though are particularly appropriate since HCE is of Nordic stock, and the most appropriate identificationof all is literary god was Ibsen and his play. The masterbuilder provides perhaps the most potent guilty father-figure of them all—Harvard Solness, who climbs a tower he has built at the request of a young woman, he loves and stuck by god he defies and figuratively rivals, falls from it to his death. An essential lesson of Finnegans Wake, if we can talk about "lessons" in connection with so undidactic a work, is that sin and creation go together, and that 11 which compliments 32 stands not only for rising but for raising. HCE has sinned, as have all men, but the sin has driven him out of the garden of Eden only to plant him in the urge to create Eden—substitutes cities and civilasations. The fall is paradoxically, a happy pne "a felix culpa", said St Augustine. Joyce planting HCE'S sin in Phonix Park puns on this with his "o Phoenix culprit".

Broadly speaking then HCE plays man the father and creator, Bygmester or master builder, ultimately he is identified with what he creates the city itself. But the creator need nature as his inspiration and consort, and cities are built on rivers. This brings us to the dream function of HCE'S wife, Ann whose dream name is Anna Livia Plurabelle the Anne Liffey (only femine river in Europe) on which Dublin stands. The "Plurabella" indicates her beauty and plurality (she contains all women). Alp conveys her natural majesty (she is bigger than any tower the bygmester can raise) snf the rough;y triangular configuration of a mountain turns her into a piece of eternal geometry she is our "geometer", or Earth mother. A triangle ALP suggests triune form she is wife, she is widow, but she is also daughter. Isobel is contained in her as is Kate the cleaning woman, praiser of days gone by, but HCE'S dream assigns to her chiefly the part of living woman and wife, protecoress of her children and of the reputation of her reviled and traduced husband, though she flowes, she is the symbol of the unchanging, while her lord, like all men, is capable of assuming many forms. Her mystery is the mysteryof all rivers the spring is different from the mouth that opens to the ocean, but both are the same water, and it is from the rivers death in the sea that the reality of new birth in the hills (the renewing rain clouds blown inland from the coast) is derived for ever and ever. As for the twin sons, they illustrate a sort of tragic comedy dialetic which owes a good deal to the Italian philosopher Giordano Bruno (1548-1600), the hertic from Nola who (in other words of Stephen Dedlaus in A Portrait Of An Artist As A Young Man) was "terribly burned". Bruno the Nolan taught the opposite principles are eventually reconciled, in heaven if not on Earth and much of Finnegans Wake deals with the clashof teo brothers unconsciously endeavouring to be made one, to flow back into the unifying father who begot their opposite natures. Joyce Hibernicises Bruno the Nolan in to "Browne and Nolan", the names of the Dublin printers who published his first peice of Juvenilia, and he contrives other punning tropes to allude to the Brunonian theory "father son Browne Podre Don Bruno", "Bruno Nowlan", "Brohan . . . N. Ohion", "Brownes berrow in nolandsland", "Bruin and Noselong". The tragedy of HCE'S two son's lies in the fact that each of his sons are only half the man his father was; neither is fit to supersede the father in task of ruling the community. They appear usually as Shem the penman and Shaun the postman; the first writes the words and the second delivers them, generally in a distorted and deloused form. Shem is the artist, and his most typical manifestation is of James Joyce himself ("Shem" is the Irish form of James)—the man who can make the dead speak but it totally incapable of coming to terms with the living, the exile who is cut off from action. Shaun (who owes a little to James Joyces brother Stanislaus) is a born demagogue and missionary, a kind of sham Christ at home in the world of action but aware that he lacks the creative spark that is needed to fire the spark of rule. They hate each other, but their fights are really avain attempt to become synthetised into a whole capable of bearing the burdent of govemnet. Anything either does tend to be cancelled out by the action of the other; When Shaun is accused of his fathers crime. Shem bears false witness against him, and the four judges, remembering the Brunonian thesis, return a verdict of "Nolans Brumans"—the accused gets off scot free. The struggles of Shem and Shaun find an eternal archetype in the war between Lucifer and Michael the Archangel "mick verses Nick" but we are not inclined, despite the pressure of orthodoxy, to take sides. Neither is loveable, both are pitiable. Their dissonance sounds only that our ears may long for the unison of the father. On the plane of symbolic botany, Shem may have a little life in him, since sometimes he is presented as a "stem", but this cannot compare with the huge world tree that grows out of HCE and ALP. As for Shain, he is not even alive—a mere stone on the river bank. In Shaun, the fathers authority is debased to a set of fossilized maxims, wheras Shem drawn to the mother, drinks in a little of her flowing life. If we are going to prefer one to the other, we are better opting for Shem. After all Shem wrote the book.

These then are the main characters of Finnegans Wake although later i will go into more detailed description of each character, to help you understand them better. HCE names the play, and the casting as automatic. If he the heavy lead, is Adam, Shaun is Abel and Shem Cain, and ALP must be mother Eve. If HCE is King Leary, Shaun must be the missionary St Patrick, Shem his archdruid opponent, and Isobel is St Bridget. Not all the character need to be employed at the same time; Hce is out of the troup for a great part of the book, and then his guilt, as well as his authority can be transferred wholly to the sons. Shaun can be Parnell, Shem Piggot and Isobel Kitty O'Shea. On the whole ALP has a little more time for acting; being a river is very nearly s full time job. But now, having presented the actors, we must see how they fit into the vast single drama which encloses so many lesser ones; we must enter the Viconian Amphitheatre.

## (III)

We have mentioned everybody but Finnegan himself, and yet it is his wake that gives the book its title. Now we must not speak of Finnegans Wake, however, but of "Finnegan's Wake" a different title all together, though the difference cannot be made apparent to the ear. "Finnegan's Wake" is a New York Irish ballad which tells of the death of Tim Finnegan, a builder's labourer who, fond of the bottle falls from his ladder at a great height. His wife family and friends sit mourining and drinking round his laid-out corpse, but soon a fight breaks out;

Micky Maloney raised his head,
When a gallon of whiskey flew at him;
It missed, and falling on the bed
The liquor scattered over Tim.
"och, he revives see how he raises"
And Timothy, jumping up from the bed,
Sez, "whirl your liquor around the Blazes
Souls to the devil D'ye think i'm dead?"

The ballad may be taken as demotic resurrection myth and one can see why, with its core of profundity wrapped round with the language of ordinary people, it appealsed so much to Joyce. His book starts with this story, but Tim Finnegan is elevated to the rank of devine master builder, a fabulous pre historic hero hardly seperable from Finn MacCool, giant leader of the Ossianic epic poetry. Fallen, his head is the head of Howth, his body lies under the city of Dublin and his feet may be located near Chapelizod. In the dream drama there is only one man to play him, and that of course is HCE, but we must not at this stage confuse a performance with an identification. Finnidan dies his wake is held, and during the wake we are given a survey of his mythical world, but also of the new world of true history which is to come after him. In other words Finnegan stands for the first phrase of the Viconian cycle, the rule of god and the heros, but with his thunderous fall and death, we must look foward to a coming of an age of purley human rule we expect the arrival of an un heroic family man, somebody like Humphrey Chimpden Earwicker. When Finnegan found out that the legend may be fulfilled, he woke up spilling his whiskey, he is told to lie down again; arrangements have been made for the second phrase of the Viconian cycle, and that Finnegan would only distrupt the pattern. Let him sleep until the wheel comes full circle and the kettledrums drum in a return of theocratic rule.

So now HCE, playing himself, arrives from overseas and the vague mixed tale of his fall is told. It seems that three soliders saw him in Pheonix Park, apparently exhibiting himself to two innocent Irish girls (Isobel in her dual form, mixed up with the two Colleens on the arms of the city of Dublin). A caddish pipe smoking man named apparently Magrath passes oin, greatly garbled and expanded, the story of HCE'S misdemeanour to his wife;she tells it further expanded to a priest soon it is all over Dublin, and a bard called Hosty makes a scurrllous ballard about poor HCE, now christened Persse O'Reiliy. He is accused of every sin in the calander and is eventually brought to trial. Locked up in prison, reviled by a visiting American (so that he should appear a disgrace to the new world as well as the old) he is at length shoved into a coffin and buried deep under Lough Neogh.

All this is told in hints and rumours; HCE'S fall is an ancient as Adam's. Among the rumours is one about a letter written by HCE'S wife ALP (she signed the letter a laughable party), in which is defence is set at length; he has enemies, his crime was greatly exaggerated, he was a good husband and father. Meanwhile as with Parnell, King Arthur and Finn MacCool himself, it is whispered abroad that HCE is not really dead, that his indomitable spirit is uncontainable by any grave, however deep and watery. He thrusts up shoots of energy; there are quarries, wars break out. The theme of the opposed brothers now make its first full length appearance. Hce's guilt has become a matter of living moment once more, and it seems to attach to Shaun (called now for some obscure reason, Festy King). But the trial is a far less massive affair than HCE's abd tge appearance of Shem as a witness discreditable and discredited—makes the whole issue fizzle out. We are asked to forget about the brothers for a brief space and to concentrate on ALP's letter in oither words to continue to concern ourselves with big HCE legend.

The letter scratched up from a middle heap by a hen called Belinda, becomes the object of mock scholarship. Certain people and places are mentioned in it, and a chapter is devoted to a quiz of twelve questions on these. Shaun now reveals himself into a valuable schoolmaster. He gives a lengthy lecture on the theme of fraternal opposition, illustrating this with certain parables. Shaun himself appears in the first of them disguised as Pope Adrian lV, the only English Pope whi gave his blessing to Henry 11's annexationof Ireland, since this would bring the old Irish church under the wing of Rome. Shem stands for the old faith, embodied in St Lawrence O'Tool,

Bishop of Dublin at the time of the English conquest. We have in fact two forms of the Christian faith which the domineering spirit of Shaun will not suffer to live peaceably side by side. One has to overcome the other. A more homely parable concerns Burrus and Caseous? (butter and cheese), bioth products of the same substance, the paternal milk, who are the rivals for the loveof Margareen. The conclusions is the reconciliation between the brothers is not possible, that Shaun and Shem must stand accursed, unloved, unprotected.

We are then presented with a full length portrait of Shem and at the same time introduced to the big food theme which plays such an important part of the story. At the Finnegan, the flesh to be devoured was that of a dead hero; with the coming of the brothers. It is the substance of the father HCE which must nourish the new rulers. Shem eats all the wrong food; he will not take the Irish salmon of Fin MacCool, for instance, but prefers some foreign much out of a tin. Shem is low un Irish, writer of nasty books, but he flourishes the lifewand, makes the dead speak. He stands for living mercy, while Shaun is all dead justice. It is through Shem that we are able to approach ALP, the living mother; she composed the letter, but Shem penned it. And so we move to the final chapter of the first section, in which Anna Livia Plurabelle's love story is told, and in which she describes the spoils of the battle which destroyed her lord's reputation in the form of gifts to her 111 children, thus sweetening memory and allaying the residue of his guilt.

The second section of the book is concerned mainly with the children of HCE and ALP, who prepare for great work ahead in games and study. Shaun is now called Chuff and Shem is called Glugg. Chuff is an angel and Glugg is the devil, and they fight bitterly, while the twenty nine girls (who all loved Chuff and not Glugg), look on dancing, singing teasing Glugg with unanswerable riddles. After play come lessons time, and a whole chapter is arranged to accomadate the text of the boys lessons, with footnotes and marginal comments. The substance of the lesson is comprehensive, covering the secret doctrines of the cabala, as well as the subjects of the medieval trivium and quadrivium. At the end of it all the children fly off to their new world, where they sent a letter of greeting to the old decaying world which they have superseded.

But now surprisingly, and in a chapter of great length, we come face to face again with HCE. This time in his capacity of innkeeper. His customers the twelve and the four very prominent represent the entire human community, whose purpose it is to discredit HCE in all sort of oblique ways, through the tales he obsecurly figures, through a television programme, through accounts of imperialistic wars. Even his alleged sin in Phonix Park is sniggeringly hinted at, and Hce is forced to defend himself, pointing out that all men are sinners. But he is reviled and rent, and the sound of a mob coming to linch him led by hosty singing a threatening rant, makes him clear and lock the bar. But it is all revealed as depressed hallucinations a dream within a dream and HCE, alone in his bar save for the four old men, who lurk in the shadows, drinks up the dregs from the abandoned pots and glasses and collapses. In a stupor on the floor, he dreams of hiself as King Mark, whose destined bride

Tristram has taken, an old spent man who must handover the future to his son.

The next section is all about Shaun. In the first chapter he presents himself to the people-sly, demagogic, totaly un trustworthy, obsessed with hatred for his brother and ready with another parable to figure the forth the enmity—a charming tale called "The ondt and the Gracehoper", in which he himself is the industrious insect, while Shem, the irresponsible artist, fritters the hours away in the sunshine. But Shaun is more ready to admit to himself now that hisown extrovert philosophy is insufficient, that the life of the "gracehoper" has its points. Shaun can rule over space, but he cannot, like the artist, "beat time". Sooner or later, when Shaun's rule collapses, we shall be forced back to the father, im whom both dimensions meet and make a rounded world. Shaun rolls off in the form of a barrel; he has filled himself with the food that is his father, but it has not nourished him, he is becoming a big bloated emptiness.

But, his name has changed to Jaun, he is ready to appear as a king of seedy Christ to take the twenty nine girls of St Bride's reeling off questionable homilies to them, eventually—sensing that the time for his departure is not far off summoning the holy host (Shem) to act as proxy bridegroom to his consort the church, who is of course, Isobel. The daughters of Erin weep over him as over the dead god Osiris. His third chapter shows him as a pathetic wreck, vast, inflated, lying supine on a hill rightly re-christened yawn. The four old men question him, but they are not interested in his own essence from which he derives; they ask about HCE and his ancient sin, the work he did, the world he built. But yawn is evasive and the task of inquisition is handed over to four bright young transatlantic brain trusters. Eventually, through a spiritualistic medium and crackling with static, the authentic voice of HCE comes through. He confesses his sins, but affirms his deathless love for his consort ALP, whom he has adorned with a city. And so the dream in the bedroom over the public bar dissolves and, through the dreaming eyes of the author, we see the decadent times which Shaun's rule has brought about figured in the sterile rituals of marital sex. Mr and Mrs Porter copulate, their shadows on the blind flash, the act to the world, but it brings no message of renewed fertility. These bad times, we the readers are living in them. It is for the ricorso, the crack of devine thunder which will bring us to our knees to contemplate the return of a theocracy.

In the final section, a single chapter, Sunday morning comes and we turn our eyes to the East looking for hope in an alien order of wisdom. The innkeeper goes to sleep again, and he dreams of his son Shaun as he may be, an agent of theocracy, a bringer of the word of god. The boy Kevin appears as St Kevin, and we are lead back to one genuine historical year in the whole chronicle 432 AD, the year of the coming of St Patrick. He refutes the messed up idealism of Archdruid (who is also Bishop Berkely) and speaks out the Christian message in a main voice. But the last word is neither God's nor man's; it is womans. We are given at last the full text of ALP'S letterand she herself a river now dreams herself on to her death and consummation in her father the sea. Her day is done. She was once the young bride from the hills, a roll passed onto her daughter; now, with the filth of man's city on her back, shemust seek renewal through annihilation; she will return at length to her source in rain-clouds blown in from the sea. The hope of re-birth, for the wprld as well as the river, is at one fulfilled. The last sentence of the book is incomplete; to finish it we must turn back to the beginning again. And then we are led onto pursue the great cycle once more, the neverending history of man, sinner and creator.

*Erica Gregory*

# (IV)

So much for the story of Finnegans Wake, but the story is inseperable from the language in which Joyce tells it. It is the language, not the theme, which makes for difficulty and difficulty is intentional. The purpose of a dream is to obscure truth, not reveal it; reality comes in flashes of lightening out of dark clouds of fantsy, but it is the fantasy which it is the author's duty to record. Joyce is presenting us with a dream, not with a piece of Freudian or Jungian dream—exegesis. Interpretation is up to us; he makes up the riddles, not the answers. But, as with so much of Joyce, a key to the language awaits us in popular literature; the verbal techniques comes straight out of Lewis Carroll. HCE is identified with that great faller Humpty Dumpty and it is Humpty Dumpty who explains the dream language of "jabberwacky". What Humpty Dumpty calls "portmanteau-words" like "slithy", which means "sly" and "lithe" and "slimy" and "slippery" all at the same time are very legitimate devise for rendering a quality of dreams. In dreams, identities shift and combine and words ought to mirror this. Walking life tells us that out of a buried body new life will spring, but it is our custom to work out the life—death cycle in terms of logical propersition. The language of Finnegans Wake takes a short cut in the rendering of such notions, and the word "corpse" sums up in one syllable a whole resurrection sermon. Waking language is mode out of time and space, the gaps between the substances that occupy the one and the events that occupy the other; In dreams there are no gaps.

The technique of Finnegans Wake represents a sort of glorification of the pun, the ambiguilty which makes us see a fundermaental, but normally disregarded, identification in a burst of laughter or a nod of awe. The very title is a complex pun, one missed by printers and editors who restore the apostrophie which Joyce deliberately left out. The primary meaning is one with an apostrophy—"the Wake of Finnegan"—but as we read the book, we find a secondary meaning assuming a greater and greater part in the sesmantic complx; "the Finnegans wake up", the cycle is renewed". The very name contains the opposed notions of completion and renewal; "fin" or "fine" (French, Italian) and "again". One we understood the title, we are already starting to understand the book

Joyce's puns are more complicated than those of Lewis Carroll and they tend to sort of progressive transformation which, though baffling is shown to be quite logical in a dreaming way. One the first page of the book we meet the expression "tauftauf". The german word for "baptise" is "taufen:, the tudor of St Patrick was St Germanieus and it is dreamily appropriate that the patron saint of Ireland should use the german to the point to the continuity, as well as the supra nation essence, of Christian evangelism. But later on "tauftauf" becomes a name "toffy tough"— and finally (appropriate for baptism) it turns to "douche douche", very little of the original is left, and only the surface meaning and the reduplication show us that this is meant to be a pun at all. The use of the German word is bound, by the way, to disturb those readers who can accept puns but only know them in English. Joyce was a great linguist, at home in most of the tongues of Europe, and his word play is multilingual ranging from Erse to Sanskrit, though rarely further East. The language of Finnegans Wake has been aptly called "Eurish" a basis of

Irish. English with a superstructure of Aryan loan words. This is not sheer wantonness; the dream is, so to speak, a caucasion one, and the hero HCEis a type of all Westward migrating conqueros. As all the rivers flow into Anna Livia Plurabella, so all Aryans—peaking races enrich the blood of her husband. The language of his dreams has shown this.

Joyce parodies where he does not pun (where the bus stops there stops i), and where he does neither he still contrives to lend his language an extra dimesnsion of meaning. Most of the devices he uses are demonstrated in the opening line of the book, a sort of advertise crammed with themes destined for strenuous development once the story starts. Thus, the "riverrun, past Adams and Eves" is a bit of pure topography on one level (the river is Liffey, Adam and Eves is the church on its bank), but on another level it is the beginning of human history, the first hint of the fall of man and the polarity of the sexes, "Sir Tristram, Violar D'amores" is both the Tristram of Arthurian legend and the Sir Almeric Tristram who founded St Lawerence family and buil Howth Castle, he plays love songs on the Viola D'amore, he violates both Iseult and his honour. "Wielderfight" means "fight again" (German weider means again) and also "wield weapons in wild fight." The "penisolate war" is the war of the pen in isolation (Shem, artist in exile), the sexual war, with its thrust of the penis, and the peninsular was which (Wellington and Napoleon) is a type of the struggle of brothers locked in mutal hate. The reference to the "doubling" on the river Oconee in Laurens country, Georgia is an accurate piece of geographical information; there is a town called Dublin on that stream and in that country, Joyce is concerned with hinting with the events of history repeats themselves, not only in time but in space as well; what happens in the old world happens also in the new, (The gypsie word "gorgio" means "youngerster", implying that the American Dublin is a child of the Irish one, as Shaun founder of the new worlds, is a child of HCE), "mishe mishe" is the erse for "i am, i am "St Bridget, as a mother of Ireland affirming her immortality. "Thuartpeatrick" is "Thou art Patrick", echoing "Thou art Peter", and also an identification of Irelands father saint with the "peat rick" of the land itself. "not very yet, though venison after had a kidscad buttendeda a bland ols Isaac" is crammed with layers ofmeaning, Isaac Butt was ousted from the leadership of the Irish national Party by Parnell (the wheels turns; one leader supersedes another). The cadet or younger son, Jacob disguised in Kidskin as hairier Esau dupes his blind father Isaac, makes him the butt of his deceit. "venissoon" is "very soon" but also "venison" (appropriate in the biblica contet of goatsnd burnt offerings) and it modulates the harmo to swi and Stella and Vanessa, "not yet though alls fair in vanessy, were sosie sesthers wrath with twone nathandjoe." The last word is an anagram of swifts Christian name, Jonathan, presenting him as Nathan (wise) and Joseph (untemptable) two in one.Susannah, Esther and Ruth are the "Sosie Sesthers Wroth" all in the Bible, all young girls champed at by old men'd passion but also (in Vanessy is Inverness) three sisters who tempted and enchanted Macbeth. As two girls can be three as well as one (all are summoned up in HCE'S daughter), so Ham, Shem and Jophet can be Jhem and Shen. Noah's sons brewing by "arc light" (rainbow light, arc de ciel or Regenbogen) the liquor which willmake Noah drunk and naked (protectionless) before them.

Should one go as far in gigging out strata of meaning? Only is one wishes to; Finnegans Wake is a puzzle, Just as a dream is a puzzle, but the puzzle element is less important than the thrust of the narrative and the shadowy majestiq of the characters. We conget along very well with a few key words and the general drift, and when are eyes grow bewildered with strange roots and incredible compounds why, then we can switch on our ears. It is astonishing how much of the meaning is conveyed through music; the art of dim sighted Joyce is like that of Milton mainly auditory. But if we still dispose to curse the book as breaking those laws of intelligibility subscribed to by Nevil Shute and Ian Fleming, we ought to remind ourselves that a book about a dream would be false to itself if it made everything as clear as daylight. If it woke up and because rational it would no longer be Finnegan's Wake. To complain that itis mixed up, over-fluid, maddeningly complex bursting at the seams with symbols, is to say that it resembles a dream not a derogation but a compliment. Whether we want dreams or not is another matter, but we seem to. Since we willingly spend a third of all our life in sleep.

We have been serious about Finnegan's Wake and we must remain serious about any work that took seventeen years to write, but let us guard against being like Hemingway's bloody owl, solemn. This is like Ulysses, a great comic version, one of the few books in the world that can make us laugh aloud on nearly everypage. Its humour is of that traditional king, alive in Rabelais, still kicking in Sterne, which modulates easily from the farcical to the sublinae and from the witty to the pathetic a humour not much found in our brutal, sentimental and facetious age, hence a humour much needed. It seduces us into the acceptance of a view of humanity as realistic as that as Dante, and quiet as optimistic. Finnegan's Wake appeared on the eve of Armageddon when things looked their blackest for the entire human race. The 32 seemed embossed on every bullet, the 11 two sticks burnt in the ultimate fire, but man rose again. In Joyce annihilation becomes "abhihilisation" the creation of new life ab nihilo, from the egg of nothing. As long as the race exists, Finnegan's Wake will remain of its big pertinent codices. The corpse is "cropse". Or to borrow Elliot's borrowing, "sin is behavely but all shall be well and all manner of thins shall be well". This is not the philosophy of Shaun, the vapid liberal demagogue, but the faith of HCE who "here comes everybody" is suffering man himself.

Critics disagree on whether or not discernable characters exist in Finngegans Wake. For example Grace Eckley argues that Wakean characters are distinct from each other and defends this with explaining the dual narrators, the "us" of the paragraph, as well as Shem and Shaun distinctions. While Margot Norris argues that the characters are fluid and inetchanable. Supporting the latter stance, Van Hulle finds that the characters in Finnegans Wake are rather "archetypes or character amalgams, taking different shapes", and Riquelme similarly refers to the books cast of mutsble characters as "proteon". As early as in 1934, in 1934, in response to the recently published excerpt. "The mookse and the gripes ", Ronald Symond argued that the characters in the work in progress, in keeping with the space time chaos in which they live, change identity at will. At one time they are persons, at another rivers, stones or trees, at another personifications of an idea, at another they are lost and hidden in the actual texture of the prose, with an ingenuity for surpassing that of crossword critics identify the books main protagonists; for example, while most find consenseus that festy king, who appears total in 1.4, is A hce type, not all analysts agree on this for example Anthony Burgess believes him to be Shaun . . .

However, while characters are in constant state of flux; constantly changing names, occupations and physical attributes, a re occurring set of core characters or character tyoes are discernible. During the composition of Finnegans Wake, Joyce used signs or so called Sigla rather than names to designate these character amalgams of types. In a letter to his Maeceanas, Harriet Shaw Weaver (March 1924,) Joyce made a list of these Sigla. For those who argue for the existence of distinguishable characters the book focuses on the Earwicker family, which consists of father, mother twin sons and daughter.

Humphrey Chimpden Earwicker (HCE)

Kitcher argues for the father HCE as the book's main protagonist stating that he is the dominant figure throughout. His guilt, his shortcomings his failures pervade the entire book, Bishop states that while the constant flux of HCE'S character and attributes may lead us to consider him as an "anyman". He argues that "the sheer density of certain repeated details and concerns allowing us to know that he is particular, real Dubliner". The common critical consensus of HCE'S fixed character is summerized by Bishop as being "an older protestant male, or Scandinavian lineage, connected with the pubkeeping business somewhere in the neighbourhood of Chapelizod, who has a wife, a daughter and two sons.

HCE is reffered to be literally thousands of names throughout the book; leading Terence Kilieen to argue that in Finnesgans Wake "naming is a fluid and provisional process", names as "Haromphreyld", and as a consequence of his initials "here comes everybody". These initials lend them to phrase after phrase throughout the book, for example appearing in the books opening sentence as "Howth Castle and Envisions". As the work progresses the names by which he may be referred to become increasingly abstract (such as Finn MaCool, Mr Makeall Gone", or Mr Porter).

Some Wake critics see Finnegan, whose death, wake and resurrection are the subject of the opening chapter, as either a prototype of HCE, or another one of his manifestations. One of the reasons for this close identification is that Finnegan is called a "man of had, cement and edifices" and "like Haroun Childeric Eggberth", identifying him with the initials HCE. Parrinder for example states that "Bygmester Finnegan is HCE", and finds that his fall and resurrection foreshadow "the fall of HCE early in book 1 (which is) paralleled by his resurrection towards the end off 111.3, in the section originally called "Haveth Childers everywhere", when (HCE) ghost speaks forth in the middle of a séance.

Anna Livia Plurabella (ALP)

Patrick McCarthy describes HCE'S wife ALP as the river woman whose presence is implied in the "riverrun" with which Finnegans Wake opens and whose monologue closes the book. For over six hundred pages, however, Joyce presents Anna Livia to us almost exclusively through other characters, mush as in Ulysses we hear that Molly Bloom has to say about herself only in the last chapter. The most extensive discussion of ALP comes in chapter 1.8, in which hundreds of names of rivers are woven into the tale of ALP'S life. Similarly hundreds of city names are woven into "Haveth Childers Everywhere", the corresponding passage at the end of 111.2 which focuses on HCE. As a result it is generally contended that HCE personifies the Viking—founded city of Dublin and his wife ALP personifies the river Liffey, on who's banks the city was built.

The children Shem, Shaun and Issy.

ALP and HCE have a daughter Issy whose personality is often split (represented bu her mirror twin). Parrinder argues that "as a daughter and sister, she is an object of secret and repressed desire both to her father and her two brothers". These twin sons of HCE and ALP consists of a writer called Shem the penman and a postman called Shaun the post, who are rivals for replacing their father and for there sister Issy's affection. Shaun is portrayed as a dull postman conforming to society's expectations, while Shem is a bright artist and sinister experiments, often perceived as Joyce's alter ego in the book. Hugh Staples finds that Shaun "wants to be tought of as a man about town a snappy dresser. A glutten and a gourmet . . . He is not happy in his work, which is that of a messenger or a postman; he would rather be a priest. Shaun's sudden and somewhat unexpected promotion to thr book's central character in Book 111 is explained by Tindall with the assertion that "having disposed of old HCE, Shaun is becoming a new HCE".

Like their father, Shem and Shaun are reffered to by different names throughout the book, such as "caddy and Primas," "Mercius and Justius", "Doplh and Kevin" and "Jerry and Kevin". These twins are contrasted in the book by allusions to sets of opposing twins and enimes in literature, mythology and history; such as Seti and Horus of the Osiris story; the biblical parts of Jacob and Esau, Cala and Abel, and Saint Michael and the devil equating Shaun with "Mick" and Shem with "Nick" as well as Romulus and Remus.

Minor characters

The book is also populated by a number of minor characters such as four Masters, the twelve customers, the Earwickers cleaning staff Kate and Joe, as well as more obscure characters such as "MaGrath ",Lily Kinsella, and the bell ringer "Fox Goodman".

The most commonly reacurring character outside of the Earwicker family are the four old men known collectively as "Mamalujo" (a conflation of their names; Matt Gregory, Marcus Lyons, Luke Tarpey and Johnny Mac Dougall). These four most commonly serve as narrators, but they alsoplay a number of active roles in the text, such as when they serve as the judges in the court case of 1.4 or the inquisitors who question Shaun in 111.4. Tindall summerizes the role that these old men play as those of the four masters, the four Evangelists and the four providences of Ireland (Matthew from the North is Ulster, Mark from the South is Munster; Luke from the East is Leinster and John from the West is Connaught"). According to Finn Fordham, Joyce related to his daughter in law Helen Fleischmann that "Mamalujo" also represents Joyces own family, namely his wife Nora (mama), daughter Lucia (LU) and son Giorgioe (Jo).

In addition to the four old men, there are a group of twelve un-named men who always appear together and serve as customers in Earwickers pub, gossips about his sins, Jurors at his trial and mourners at his wake. The Earwickers household also includes two cleaning staff, Kate the maid and Jow who is by turns the handyman and barman in Earwickers pub.These characters are seen bu most critics as older versions of ALP and HCE. Kate often plays the role of meseum curator as in the "willingdone Huseyroom" episode 1.1 and is recognised by her repeate motif "TIP TIP"". Jow is often reffered to by the name "Sackerson", and Kitcher describes him as "a figure sometimes playing the role of policeman sometimes a squalid derelict, and most frequently the odd job man of HCE'S inn, Kates male counterpart, who can ambiguously indicate an older version of HCE.

A PORTRAIT OF AN ARTIST AS A YOUNG MAN 1916.

"History, Stephen said, is a nightmare from which I am trying to awake." James Joyce quote from the book.

A portrait of an artist as a young man tells the story of Stephen Dedalus (also in Ulysses), a boy growing up in Ireland at the end of the nineteenth century, as he gradually decides to cast of all his social, familiar and religious constraints to live a life devoted to the art of writing. As a young boy Stephen's catholic faith and Irish nationality heavily influenced him. He attends a strict religious boarding school called Clongowes Wood College. At first, Stephen is lonely and homesick at the school, but as time passes he finds his place among the other boys. He enjoys his visits home, even though family tensions run high after the death of the Irish political leader Charles Stewart Parnell. This sensitive subject becomes the topic of furious politically charged argument over the family's Christmas dinner.

Stephen's father Simon is inept with money and the family sinks deeper and deeper into dept. After a summer spent in the company of his uncle Charles, Stephen learns that the family can not afford to send him back to Clongowes, where he grows to excel as a writer and as an actor in the student theatre. His first sexual experience with a young Dublin prostitute unleashes a storm of guilt and shame in Stephen, as he tries to recognise his physical desires with the stern catholic morality of his surrounding, for a while, he ignores his religious upbringing throwing himself with debauched abandon into a Variety of sins—masturbation,, gluttony and more visits to prostitutes among others. Then on a three day religious retreat Stephen hears a trio of fiery sermons about sins, judgement and hell. Deeply shaken the young man resolves to rededicated himself to a life change of Christian faith.

Stephen begins attending mass everyday becoming a model catholic. Obstinence and self denial. His religious devotion is so pronounced that the director of his school asks him to consider entering the priesthood. After briefly considering the offer, Stephen realises that the austerity of the priestly life is utterly incompatible with his love for sensual beauty. That day Stephen learns from his sister that the family will be moving, once again for financial reasons. Anxiously awaiting news about his acceptance to the university, Stephen goes for a walk on the beach, where he observes a young girl awaiting the tide. He is struck by her beauty and realizes in a moment of epiphany that the love and desire of beauty should not be a source of shame. Stephen resolves to live his life to the fullest and vows can not be constrained by the boundaries of his family, his nation and his religion.

Stephen moves onto the university where he develops a number of strong friendships and especially close to a young man named Cranley. In a series of conversations with his companions, Stephen works to formulate his theories about art. While he is dependant on his friends as listens he is also determined to create an independent existence, liberated from the expectations of friend and family. He becomes more and more determined to free himself from all limiting pressures and eventually decides to leave Ireland to escape them. Like is namesake, the mythical Dedalus, Stephen hopes to build himself wings on which he can fly above all obstacles and achieve a life as an artist.

Copied with permission from the James Joyce society.

# EPISODE 5

# Brady vs. Joyce

---

Now we have looked at Brady and James Joyce's backgrounds we are going to explain some very fascinating links and comparisons between the pair. This will also help you to understand how we came to our conclusion.

James Joyce is known for his complex ideas and works. He based his work on real people. This includes his family, friends and the likes of Shakespeare, Dante and Oscar Wilde.

He mapped the area of Dublin using this as the base for his book. He used a map, compass and local street directory (The Thom's Local) to invent the street and character names he used. By spending many months researching him as a person we were trying to understand and interpret his writing. We find that snippets of what he included in his life mirror that of Brady and Hindley.

Did the pair use these characters to act out scenes? It seems that people such as Maureen (Myra's Sister), David Smith and the victims were also unknowingly a part of the story they created in the environs of Gorton/Hattersley and the bleak A635 over Saddleworth Moor. There are far too many coincidences to ignore.

## Joyce

Joyce's family began to notice his genius at a young age; his education came from his life in Cork that furnished him with an encyclopaedic knowledge of local trivia. His son was later employed in to his novels; Joyce divided Ulysses in to 18 chapters or 'episodes'. At first glance much of the book seems to be unstructured and chaotic. Joyce once said that he had: "put in so many enigmas and puzzles that it will keep the professors busy for centuries arguing over what I meant". James Joyce's novel Ulysses was banned in the USA as it was seen to be obscene, 'Dubliners'—another of Joyce's work was also on the list of banned books. A mile away from his home was the City of Dublin's Public Library on Capel Street. Joyce spent much of his young life there and could quite possibly be credited as perhaps the true start of his independent education.

## Brady

Much of Brady's own education also came from the books he read in local libraries. Whilst in prison during his youth he buried himself into books. His mother said: "he came out of prison with his head in a book; many of the titles that he read were hard to come by literature and many had been banned at some time or another. Some of these books were works by The Marquis De Sade, Shakespeare and Ovid and Goethe"

## Joyce

Quotes were made about Joyce's personality and habits. One of the statements came from his own father: "he would find his own private mountain". "He could be dropped in the Sahara and he would sit and map it".

**Brady**

Brady had a deep love for landscapes and being out in the open. The Lake District and Peak District were some of his favourite places; the countryside close to his birth place being another. The photos in his albums show his love for the vast outdoors. Mapping area's just like Joyce for his plans.

**Joyce**

Even though Joyce had most attributes people envied, he struggled in other departments. After a few failed attempts to lose his virginity, he finally decided to take the plunge. His first ever sexual experience was with a local Dublin prostitute.

**Brady**

Brady was known to be a frequent visitor to the Central Station area of Greater Manchester. This area also happened to be the local gathering place of the local homosexuals. This is the area he stated he had met Edward Evan's previously. This is also Manchester's "red light district" frequented by prostitutes.

**Joyce**

Between the dates of 1900 and 1903 Joyce began scribbling in notebooks. He would write about the prose experiments he called "epiphanies", by which he meant "the sudden revelation". It is described as the moment in which "the soul of the commonest object seems to us radiant. It is a sudden spiritual manifestation (either) in the vulgarity of speech or of gesture or in a memorable phrase of the mind itself". Epiphanies are described as being given an idea from the spiritual or divine world.

## Brady

Brady stated that one afternoon when he was out he looked in a shop window he suddenly saw a "green face of death". He promised this "apparition" that he would sacrifice himself to it. What was he really seeing here? Was it his "green mist" forming? We found a book—Sir Gawain and the Green Knight. This book was translated by J.JR Tolkien and a poet called WS Merwin. In the book the character has a meeting with a green mist, a ghost that comes to the knight. The area at Ludchurch seen in the photographs is an area where the Green Chapel is supposed to be. Brady would have been attracted to this area in the Peak district. We noticed that the winking man rock at this location resembles the profile of James Joyce. Would that also be a reason in Brady's mind why he would go there? WS Merwin we know wrote the book 'The Mask of Janus' which is a book of poems. He also translated Dante's work. J.JR Tolkien has a link to Saddleworth Moor itself through a man called Ammon Wrigley—a poet whose monument stands on the hill near the area of Greenfield. This poetry could have quite easily been an interest to Brady at one time. Wrigley's poem the hill of sleep is quite an eye opener, here is the last verse.

"And they, who round one hearth, grew up.
In life to wonder wide,
Like children, all come back at last
To slumber sick by side;
And in the start calm of night,
Like wind among the grass,
I hear across their lowly graves,
The feet of angel pass.
And when can Earth to Earth return,
In fairer field of sleep;
Than where this gateway of the skies,
Looks out o'er vale and steep."
Ammon Wrigley; 1861-1946

## Joyce

Joyce was well known to mirror his work to other people. He even included other famous writers and poets in his books—despite Joyce being an established writer and poet himself. He was also a singer (even though it never gained him stardom) and loved the Opera and Folk music. His love of music also mirrored in his writing—one of his lesser known pieces was named Chamber Music. In Ulysses he also wrote a song for the character Molly Bloom (mirrored on his real life wife Nora). The song named: "Shall I Wear the White Rose?" This is also another link but will be explained more later on. Joyce wrote Finnegan's Wake whilst reading the book "Gentlemen prefer Blondes". He also wore a white coat to help his poor eyesight.

## Brady

Similarly, Brady had a well known love of Opera and Folk music. Most people who have met/corresponded with Brady know this. He sent a tape of mixed songs to one of the people who have given us snippets of information. She did not realise that looking at each song closely at the singer/writer he was giving hidden messages and codes. Unfortunately I cannot share this due to confidentiality issues as we do not have the permission from either party. Folk music is derived from the word "volk"—a German word. Folk may have a Germanic root which is unique to the Germanic languages yet Latin vulgus means, "the common people". Greenwich Village in the USA is known for its folk music festivals. We have found many links to the Greenwich Village especially with poets and singers Brady used. One of these artists being the legendary Bob Dylan. Brady gave to Hindley some music the morning of Edward Evan's murder. This was to celebrate the upcoming event as he did with all the victims. His choice of music was Bob Dylan's "It's all over baby blue". This was written and performed by himself and was featured on his "Bringing It All Back Home" album. The lyrics were heavily influenced by symbolist poetry. He wrote his lyrics in surrealism as Joyce did with his.

The Beatles influenced by Bob Dylan. They were the first to popularise the use of surrealism in lyrics and instrumentals. This is another link with The Beatles. The lyrics of the song "It's all over baby blue" will be explained later in Edward's story. He also wrote his lyrics in the same way Joyce wrote Ulysses in the stream of consciousness. Gene Pitney's "24 hours from Tulsa" was the song given to Hindley from Brady on the morning of the disappearance of John Kilbride; again this was given as a way of celebrating the upcoming events. This also links back to the Greenwich Village festival. The James Joyce Quarterly (JJQ) is a peer reviewed academic journal which was established in 1963. It covers critical and theoretical work focusing on the life, writing and reception of James Joyce. The journal publishes essays, notes, reviews, letters and a comprehensive checklist of recent Joyce related publication. The James Joyce Quarterly was established in 1963 at the University of Tulsa.

The music given to Hindley by Brady at the time of Keith Bennett's murder was Roy Orbison's "It's over". Roy Orbison was known as the voice of Greenwich Village. Greenwich Village was home to many writers—one in particular: Joseph Campbell—an expert on mythology. His book The Skeleton Key to Finnegan's Wake is surely a book Brady had read. He also wrote the book: "The Hero with a Thousand Faces". This book is used by many film directors during the plot of a hero's journey. Myra became the blonde to bring in the actress look. Just like Marilyn Monroe—she was known to have read Ulysses by Joyce. A famous photograph of her doing so was taken.

**Joyce**

'Stream of Consciousness' is a narrative device used in literature "to depict the multitudinous thoughts and feelings which pass through the mind. Another phrase used for it is "interior monologue". The term stream of consciousness was coined by philosopher and psychologist William James in 'The Principles of Psychology (1890)'.

There were more artists and writers that wrote in the form of surrealism. Surrealism is also a great connection to the 1920s ART Movement.

**Brady**

Brady's "acting out" is part of Surrealism itself. Creating a surrealist world to be in—a fantasy world he created to live in. To be like his heroes from the books he read.

**Joyce**

Joyce did not see his work as just words joined together to make sentences, paragraphs and chapters. He saw his work as individual pieces of art work, each with its own deep meaning. We can see many links in Joyce's quotes being important: "The use of everyday people as part of his art". To help realise this, Joyce rejected the literal teachings of Catholicism. He felt proper art, rather than being kinetic or static: "didn't impel you to do anything. Rather you stand away and instead of judging work, you simply behold it".

**Brady**

Brady used the church as part of his hatred for the religion and would use this as part of his art. He would leave items in church yards and desecrate the grounds by urinating on graves. Symbols mean something to him. Surrealism is part of all he loves: from Spikes Milligan's comedy to the music he listens to.

## Joyce

At the very beginning of Joyce's work his very first ideas were jotted in notebooks—The Doodle Books, later on these proved to be difficult to decipher. He would use riddles and cryptic messages that only he understood. That way nobody could steal his work as for them to do so they would have to first crack his secret code. Joyce claimed many times that Ulysses and Finnegan's Wake were full of puzzles and riddles. Idioglossia is an idiosyncratic language invited and spoken between two people. James Joyce's novel Finnegan's Wake was written using the idioglossia language. Telepathy is also used as a way to describe the cryptic writings. Many different areas around Gorton and Hattersley (Greater Manchester) were used as viewpoints. Standing Stones, Eagles Head (both on Saddleworth Moor)—and sitting upon Hindley's borrowed car: "Beholding what had happened to Pauline Reade"—while her family were looking for her. It would have looked like his art work coming to life.

## Brady

Brady wrote the plans in notebooks, one found showed Hindley and Brady were the culprits for the disappearance of John Kilbride. His name had been written among other names—mostly famous actors and musicians. This was found at 16 Wardle Brook Avenue. Brady also used to write cryptic letters to Hindley during their time in prison before she broke off all correspondence with him. Looking closely at the letters especially the ones written whilst they were in remand hold many secrets. To an onlooker the letters would look like love letters of poetry and stories written by a couple who had been ripped away from each other. What we believe is they were discussing the case and with certain stories and poetry they would be referring to different victims for possibly two reasons: firstly to get their stories straight so they would match up perfectly when they went before Judge and Jury. Secondly, to perhaps relive the horrendous murders and take each other back to the time they were inseparable.

In one of Brady's letters to Hindley while awaiting trail he wrote "do you remember the pictures of Cromwell?". We believe this may be referring to a link we have with the death of Myra's niece around the time of Oliver Cromwells birthday, the 25th April.

In the chapter about the industrial revolution, Cromwell links are explained so the above will make more sense.

Brady also quoted that he and Hindley were so close they did not always need to use the common forms of communication. Instead they would use the very sceptical art form of telepathy. They would know what the other was thinking and would be able to respond appropriately and correctly.

**Joyce**

When James Joyce was writing his piece of art he would often find a quiet area at Austria Frederich railway station. His love of trains and the atmosphere of the station would help him to concentrate on the work at hand. 'The Fate of Ulysses' was written from across the tracks. He once told a friend who accompanied him to the train station "over there, on those tracks, the fate of Ulysses was decided in 1915".

Joyce would always have his trusty suitcase with him—placing it on his lap he would use it as a desk.

**Brady**

Brady also had a great love of trains and train stations. He more than likely would have visited the stations to see the steam trains he is known to have loved. He would sit at Greater Manchester's central station with his notebooks watching what he called "The Maggots". Brady would use this area for his planning, and create his work on murder. It was also at Manchester's central station that Brady met up with Edward Evans the night that would seal the fate of the 17 year old.

He quotes this in his book 'The Gates of Janus'. He loved the nostalgia of steam. Journeys by steam train were romantic. Not far from Manchester, the train takes you to the stops of Penistone, where Wuthering Heights is located. Woodhouse Station is where the Oliver Cromwell Train visited in the 1960s many times. Woodhouse an area he and Myra were seen at in 1965.

**Joyce**

James Joyce was obsessed with the use of Alchemy in his work: the use of chemicals, shamans and magic. The words Green Vitriol are used in Joyce's 'Ulysses'—this is sulphuric acid. But Joyce creates the use of a word to bring to life the Alchemy. The God Hermes is mentioned.

Corpus Hermenticum, this is an Emerald Tablet. This refers to the GREEN again, Ireland itself. There is mention of a chemical factory. Cryptic use is all through Joyce's work.

The God Hermes is a God of travel, signposts and mileposts; he is also a shepherd and messenger and links to poetry and games. There is also mention of the God THOTH. Thoth is the God of Libraries. The esoteric symbolism and Hieroglyphs are also used. Hermetic symbolism is the way to unlock Joyce's work. The mention of a book called "The Rosie Crucian Secrets", this is a code also. Joyce's work is so complex to decipher. The ash plant is a curved stick of an auger. So magic, occultism and the Alchemy is added through his work also. The Rosicrucian Religion and a book I have found by Hargraves Jennings 1879 are important to understand. The book, Rosicrucians their Rites and Mysteries has many connetions to why symbolisim in the photograph albums show signs of freemasonry. Much I have found in this book will be explained.

**Brady**

We found Brady's love of the libraries and books goes very deep.

His knowledge of Manchester alone is extensive. He was able to map areas and create escape routes planned for himself and Myra.

He worked as a clerk in a chemical factory—starting on the 2$^{nd}$ February (Joyce's birthday—the publication date of Ulysses and parts of Finnegan's Wake). Could this be a part of the story he was creating?

The Rosie Crucian Secrets can be found in books by Dr John Dee. He was a famous Alchemist whose work is held at Chethams Library in Manchester.

There are also many photographs of Brady standing by sign posts. Brady also carried an Ash plant, a walking stick which is made from the root of the Ash tree.

Brady read books by Aleister Crowley—the English occultist. He is a mystic magician, poet and mountaineer; he was responsible for founding the religious philosophy of Thelema. As a young man he was also a member of the esoteric Hermetic Order of the Golden Dawn (much of his life influenced Brady). One book that Crowley read was The Necomonicon, an Occult book which is said to bring great evil. This book was said to be translated by no other than Dr John Dee himself. Did Brady's job at Millwards Chemical factory mean more to him? Was Brady planning his revenge on society a long time before he met Myra? He would have had many months to plan his journey—bringing in his perfect partner in crime—a mirror image of himself. He creates his own monster, just like Frankenstein.

Erica Gregory

# JOYCE

The use of the Rose and the Cross as symbols are present in both Ulysses and Finnegan's Wake.

Joyce has connections to the Rosicrucian's. W.B Yeats and Samuel Beckett both used the Rosicrucian in their work and life also. Yeats became the founding chairman of the Dublin Hermetic Society on 16 June, Bloomsday in 1885. Joyce, notoriously superstitious about birthdays and anniversaries may have seen this as important. Joyce learnt two of Yeats' Rosicrucian stories off by heart, 'The Tables of the Law' and 'The Adoration of the Magi,' Stephen Dedalus also having read both in Stephen Hero, Joyce died before completion of this book. The Rose and Cross are allusions in the works of Joyce. The mention of a Battle of the Rose, the Rose is mentioned as female and the cross male.

Rosicrusianism is a generic term referring to studies or membership within a philosophical secret society. Rosicrucianism is associated with Protestantism. They traced their philosophy and science to the Moors (as in race of people). It was influential on freemasonry as it was emerging in Scotland.

There is a Rosy Cross and this in Joyce's books mentions, the Rose growing on the cross. One of the freemasonry connections is the Rectified Scottish Rite. This society has connections to the Stuart Family. The order was resurrected by Oliver Cromwell. The White Rose lies at the centre of the cross symbol used by the society. According to Masonic writers, the Order of the Rose

Cross is expounded in a major Christian literary work that moulded the subsequent spiritual views of the western civilisation, as in the divine comedy by Dante.

Molly is, as Joyce likewise referred to Nora, a "Flower of the mountain". "I'd love to have the whole place swimming in roses" she says. *Ulysses* closes with Molly's reminiscence, "when I put the rose in my hair like the Andalusian girls used". It becomes a question of whether Molly's many roses do not, at one level, constitute 'The Rose of the World,' which Joyce encountered in Yeats books. To put it another way, we are enquiring as to whether Buck Mulligan's "primrose" waistcoat does not already imply its etymological grounding in the prima rosa, so clearly encapsulated in the "primerose" of *Finnegan's Wake*. At an abstract level, Molly Bloom, "the third person of the Blessed Trinity," is easily conceived as Joyce's rose upon the cross. Such deductive leaps would be bolstered by more concrete references to Rosicrucianism in Ulysses, which leads us firstly to the 17th century founding of the order. The Rosy Cross is also known to resemble a key.

Pour wine and dance if Manhood still have pride,
Bring roses if the rose be yet in bloom;
The cataract smokes upon the mountain side,
Our Father Rosicross is in his tomb (Yeats 1914-1964)

*Erica Gregory*

# BRADY

The use of crosses as symbols, have been found in the area of the three children already found.

Dante's Crux is a quote from Myra Hindley when she referred to their code. A Crux is a star formation which resembles a cross and rotates in an anti-clockwise direction. Dante himself a member of the Rosicrucians.

The White Rose of Yorkshire is the area we are in with our search.

Saddleworth was an area of Yorkshire until 1972.

Brady's quotes from Richard III, by Shakespeare now make sense with the "Battle of the Rose".

If we take into account the War of the Roses, the Battle fought by Richard III and his armies. This Battle between Yorkshire (White Rose) and Lancashire (Red Rose).

Brady insisted that Keith is buried in Yorkshire; He also wanted the Yorkshire police to solve this case.

Brady quoted to Myra Hindley at the trial to "Remember the Key". Myra often stated the children were the flowers in their garden.

Brady, a protestant, we know used Cromwell in his plans. Even displaying this in the use of the Cromwell helmet when riding his Triumph Tiger Cub. We also found that on Cromwell Street in Glasgow, Mickey Oates a bike shop opened in 1961, selling the Tiger Cub.

Did he also use dates of birthdays and specific events to mark with a murder? Especially using the life and work of James Joyce?

One of the items found by the group is a cross bound with rope and red electrical flex, buried with many more items in one spot we have searched.

Much from the Rosicrucian religion and the book by Hargraves Jennings seems to have been taken literally by Brady and Hindley.

The Mason symbols include:

The Rose Compass and Rosy cross are one of the same.

Compass is held in Myra's hand on a photograph by a stream.

The compass and square a Masonic symbol.

Myra also holds a square with the compass on the same photo.

The Chess Board . . . Myra displays this symbol on her mug shot. Brady plays chess all the time.

The Symbolic meaning of ropes, belts and scarfs or sash to bound the body.(Knights Templar).

Ropes and belts used by the male. The sash or scarf the female.

The use of ropes by the pair to bound the boys. The scarf is displayed in Lesley-Ann's photos taken at the time of her murder. Myra wore the scarf also in many photos.

The Rosicrucians used a cryptic code called the pigpen cipher. A code of pens and the mark of X in grids. This cipher also appears in Finnegans Wake, chapter The Rose by James Joyce.

Brady's plans hold similar grids and X marks. Something we believe he has adapted for his own secret code.

The saying from the book "They know not shame of the adult and therfore bear not the badge of men, and are not of this world really but of another world"

Quoted by Brady and Hindley to the police. "We are not of your world.

The symbol of the dog sacred to Hermes. The Cynocephalus (dog head).

Dogs used by both as part of their game. Photos of dogs in many of the albums.

The mention of human sacrifices, especially children.

This to give a God like status. To take the right hand side of the road, walk with the selfish Gods. In other words they believed to sacrifice was to give them a higher status in life.

Music especially symbolic, the rhythm connects to the heartbeat of Christ, especially Marching Music and the sound of drums.

The Green Tapes Brady made included, Green Tape one and Green Tape four, German marching music and the Christmas Carol Little Drummer Boy.

Flagellation used to "whip the body as it were into wood before we can drive the Devil from there".

Brady's books by the Marquis de Sade on the same subject.

Fire worshippers links to the worship of Lucifer. The Fire symbol and use of fire used by the religion. Lightning and electricity also.

Opening the door to the dark side is another that they both did and let in the worshipping of fire. The Fire worshippers F.W again like we have with Finnegans Wake. Brady would state about the burning of clothes and shoes, handles from weapons. Our area we search we have found the same offerings in the sheep pen. Electricity symbolised in the electrical flex he used, and lightning with the split trees he stated were important.

The symbol of the spade for male and a diamond bound by the serpent.

The shovel we have found same shape. The Diamond shape, Myra used in her clothes. Tights and dresses show this shape.

I can go into great detail about the book, but it needs to be read by yourself to get what we have. The Staffordshire connections will interest many, and the use of church yards and druid stones, all included.

Famous Rosicrucians or Freemasons

Cromwell, Dante, Davinci,Arthur Conan Doyle, Shakespeare,Shelley,Byron, Keats, Buffalo Bill, W.B Yeats, Oscar Wilde the list also goes on to film actors and is endless. Peter Sellers, Oliver Hardy amongst many. Music by Bob Dylan, The Beatles again a connection.

This cult was also used by Hitler and Aleister Crowley.

# EPISODE 6

## MYRA vs. MOLLY BLOOM

Where Brady had modelled himself on several different characters Hindley also did the same with Molly Bloom—the character in Ulysses and Nora Joyce, James Joyce's wife. There isn't quite as many links as there are for Brady but still it is unmistakable.

One link to Molly is The Wife of Bath from Chaucer's Canterbury Tales. It sounds strange that Myra stated she ran a bath at the time Lesley-Ann was murdered.

Molly's character would pose naked for pictures to make money. She also had an affair with Buck Mulligan while she was married to Bloom. Her character is described as being half Catholic and half Pagan. Joyce started that "Penelope/ Molly" revolves around "four cardinal points, the four cardinal points of a compass." She is also known as the flower of the mountain. Molly "remembers a watch that Bloom had given her during their many years of marriage". This is important between Molly and Bloom as they would give each other gifts to celebrate different eras.

Myra was known to pose naked for photographs which Brady had hoped to sell. Myra gave up her religion of being a catholic whilst with Brady and became more pagan—she later returned to being a catholic in prison.

She would collect natural herbs and plants like Sphagnum moss. She and Brady also said they took a rock from "Maggie's Wall" in Scotland—a memorial to the execution of a local woman known as a witch; they placed the stone in their back garden.

Myra would quote the children were flowers in God's garden. We have evidence the graves on the upper moor of Pauline, John and Lesley Ann, were in the North, East and West positions and placed in a 375 foot distance triangle. This leaves the cardinal point south.

Could there possibly be another victim at this point? Are the children her white roses in her garden which Brady had created for her? If they were placed at the cardinal points of Myra/Molly's body, then the missing south one would have occurred after John Kilbride.

Myra received a gold watch from Brady as a birthday present around the time of Pauline Reade's disappearance. She bought Brady gifts such as guns and rifles. The gifts were after each murder; this was a game to them. I have found in the surrealist art techniques, there is mention of a travel game called Potlatch. Games that would be classed as "Recreational", wasn't this a quote by Brady at the recent tribunal hearing?

The game of Potlatch is where two or more players have a say in what gift is given to another person. This is usually an historical person who played a role in, or had an influence on the formation of surrealism used.

The Surrealism again, part of the period of time when Joyce's Ulysses was published. The character Stephen Dedalus wears a white rose as his flower in the book 'Portrait of an Artist'. The area they chose around Greenfield at the time of the murders in the 1960's was part of the white rose of Yorkshire.

Hindley quoted "their code was a crux so to speak". The crux is a Star in Dante's Divine comedy (a journey to purgatory) which revolves around the four cardinal points of the crux (the Southern Cross).

**Bloom**

In the soliloquy of Molly Bloom the most famous part of the Ulysses book, there is mention of a one Florence Maybrick. This woman is a well known murderer who poisoned her husband James Maybrick in Liverpool 1889. She used arsenic taken from fly papers by soaking them to release the poison. James Maybrick has also been linked to the Jack the Ripper murders. This wasn't known at the time of the Moors murders, but came to light later on discovery of Maybrick's diaries. What a coincidence that is!

Molly Bloom mentions her in this part of the book. The use of poison for murder is mentioned many times in Ulysses. Rosicrucians also would create potions from nature just as a witch would.

**Myra Hindley**

As far as I know and this is only speculation, Myra's Gran Mrs Maybury, is a relative of the Maybricks in Liverpool.

The name changed to Maybury, this has yet to be confirmed, but that in itself is very important especially if factual.

We do know the poison Aconite is a symbol of the death of Leopold Blooms father. Ian Brady stated in a letter "Never trust a fly". This was included on a list of film titles and music which he sent to a member of the public. This makes us wonder what was he trying to say? Is this reference to the fact that Myra did take part in the murders, and was her method poison for a victim? Myra herself stated in her diaries that Brady tried to poison her Gran with sleeping tablets and also his dog. But was this really her?

## MYRA V MOLLY/NORA

Something we have found is James Joyce would create his characters based on real life friends and people he was influenced by. His wife Nora included. She is as we have stated the character Molly Bloom. Nora in her early life as a young girl has a boyfriend called Michael. **Michael Bodkin**—was the inspiration for Michael Furey in James Joyce's short story 'The Dead'

Michael Bodkin died young at the age of 16. This affected Nora significantly, she loved Michael.

He worked as a clerk at the local Gas Company, and was a student at Galway University. Nora Barnacle, aged fifteen, fell deeply in love with him. He reciprocated, giving her a present of a bracelet. However, Bodkin contracted TB and died. He was buried in Rahoon Cemetery on the outskirts of town.

## MYRA HINDLEY

Her friend Michael Higgins died at the age of 13 years. He drowned in a reservoir 14th June. Coincidence here Cromwells Battle of Naseby the same date.

Myra wasn't with him but this death affected her deeply. She stated she had blamed herself for his death; she should have been there to save him.

He is buried in Gorton Cemetery. This grave is where the Group, whilst attending the neglected grave, found the remains of black leather, from a shoe. This is now in the hands of a forensic expert. We planted bulbs and flowers at the grave.

Did Myra use her dead friend as part of her disgusting act? The statue next to Michael's grave is significant. We feel this point to the Moors and the position of the victims bodies. Myra was given a gift also from Michael, the rosery he held in his hand in his coffin.

ULYSSES James Joyce.

The 17th episode of 'Ulysses by James Joyce's novel known as "Ithaca", is written in the form of a catechism. Catechisms are doctrinal manuals often in the form of questions followed by answers to be memorized, a format used in non-religious or secular contexts as well.

MYRA.

Would quote that she had gone back to the teachings of Catechism. She also stated that her mother made her go to church to learn these.

Was she really saying that she had memorized this chapter as part of the plans Brady had made. That this was the Key he was referring to. This chapter holds many keys we can link.

# EPISODE 7

'The flower that smells the sweetest is shy and lowly'.
William Wordsworth.

# Pauline Reade

---

Pauline Reade lived at 9 Wiles street in Gorton Greater Manchester, with her mother Joan, father Amos and brother Paul.

After leaving school Pauline became an apprentice at the bakery where her father also worked. They would both rise very early in the morning and walk the short distance together to Sharples Bakery in Gorton's shopping thoroughfare in cross lane. Pauline and her dad Amos were extremely close. She even attended a work's dance in July 1963 with her dad in London.

In December 1962 her picture appeared in the local paper the Gorton Reporter for all the right reasons; she was one of the winners in a Christmas cake competition. She was over the moon to have won and was delighted to have her face smiling out of the paper. She would proudly show everyone she knew the article and even people she didn't know.

Pauline was a very pretty young lady with a slim figure; she had lovely dark brown hair which matched perfectly with her deep blue eyes that always seemed to have a twinkle in them.

At the tender age of 16 Pauline was turning into a stunning outgoing young lady, She loved singing and dancing, writing poetry and above all baking.

She spent many hours with her friends enjoying life. She loved going on holidays to Butlins with her family.

Pauline was also known to have dated David Smith when they were both young teenagers, David then went on to marry Myra Hindley's younger sister Maureen. David Smith was only 14 when Pauline disappeared. Pauline and her family lived 2 doors down from him.

Maureen Hindley, Myra's little sister was friends with Pauline even though were not what you would class as close. It is believed it was through Pauline, Maureen met David Smith although they did not start dating immediately.

Pauline had many friends most she had known all her life, from school and the close knit community she came from. Her best friend was a girl named Pat who lived in nearby Benster Street, the young girls could often be found in each other's bedroom's trying on different outfits, deciding what to wear for which ever dance they were attending, they were always keen to be dressed alike.

Pauline and her brother Paul were very close and spent many hours together, Pauline singing along to Paul playing his guitar. Paul wasn't the only musically talented member of the Reade family; Amos played the piano and would often play soothing music in their small lounge. Even though Amos was an excellent pianist he struggled to teach Pauline how to play so she was taking lessons from one of their neighbours.

On the 12th July 1963 Pauline had just finished her evening meal of fish and chips. Her brother Paul was out at the cinema with some friends, and her dad Amos at the pub, he returned at 7.30pm and had a fish and chip supper.

Pauline was stood looking in the mirror which hung above the fireplace putting the finishing touches to her makeup. Joan approached her daughter from behind and placed a gold locket around her neck, Pauline was thrilled to be wearing the chain as she knew it was one of her mum's prized possessions. She wore a pink and gold dress, white shoes a fitted powder blue coat and a pair of white gloves. Pauline popped ten shillings into her purse and was ready to leave.

Earlier that day on her way home from work at the bakery Pauline had called upon two of her friends to see if they were still attending a dance with her that evening, but both girls parents had refused to allow them to attend because they had discovered alcohol would be available at the dance. Pauline had begged her mum to try to persuade the other girl's parents to allow them to go. Pauline and Joan left the house firstly they called at Barbara Jepson's house on Taylor Street to speak to Barbara's mum but she would not give in and let her daughter go.

Secondly they called on Linda Bradshaw in Bannock street {a few doors away from Hindley and Brady} and walked away with the same response.

Pauline decided to go to the dance alone; she told her mum she was bound to know somebody at the dance. It's unclear as to why Joan and Amos allowed Pauline to attend the dance knowing alcohol would be available, was it the fact they trusted Pauline not to drink? Or did they trust their daughter to have a drink knowing that she would be responsible and not drink excessively?

Joan walked with her daughter to the corner of the street and waved her off as she began the short walk to the dance. When Pauline left she was unaware two of her friends Pat and Dorothy had seen her leave and did not believe she would attend the dance alone so they decided to follow her to see would.

As they neared the club the two girls decided to take a short cut so they would get there before Pauline, eager to see if she was brave enough to enter the club alone. As Pauline approached Froxmer Street they took a shortcut as planned knowing Pauline would not take this route as it takes you away from the main roads which Pauline always stuck to when alone to stay safe, little did she know this strategy would not keep her safe that evening.

Elsewhere Hindley was driving through the Gorton area in her Mini Van with her partner in love and crime Brady following closely behind on his beloved motorcycle. They were both on a mission to carry out Brady's fantasy of committing the perfect murder. They had a plan in mind,

Myra was to drive around with Brady following and if he saw a potential victim he would flash his headlights to alert her of his choice. Brady and Hindley left Bannock Street around 7.45pm to begin their search for prey.

Part way down the road Hindley noticed a young girl; it was a girl she knew well. The young girl was Pauline Reade. The headlights from the Tiger Cub reflected in Hindley's rear-view mirror. Hindley knew if she ignored Brady he would be extremely cross and she would end up on the receiving end of his punishment. So on went the indicators and Hindley pulled over to the side of the road just ahead of Pauline.

Meanwhile back at the Railway workers social club Pat and Dorothy were waiting for Pauline wondering why she had not yet arrived, even with them taking the shortcut she should still have arrived at the dance by that time. After a while of waiting they decided to leave and go home they came to the conclusion Pauline must have changed her mind about going alone and had probably returned home.

Back on Froxmer Street Hindley wound down the Mini Vans passenger window to call to Pauline, asking if she wanted a lift to her destination. Because Pauline knew Hindley she accepted the lift and got into the Mini Van. Hindley explained to her she had lost a white glove while picnicking on the Moors with Brady, she explained the glove had sentimental value to her and she would greatly appreciate Pauline going to the moors to help her look for it. When Pauline explained she was supposed to be going to a local dance at the Social Club Hindley replied it shouldn't take too long to look for the glove as it was only a small area to search and she would have her back at the dance with plenty of time to spare. Hindley also told Pauline if she could help look for the missing glove she would reward her with a few popular music records.

They drove off through the streets of Stalybridge onto the bleak A635 through Saddleworth, the road Pauline would never return from.

Once parked up in a lay-by Hindley explained they had to wait a few minutes for Brady to come and help in the search. A few minutes later the familiar headlights of the Tiger Cub came into view. Hindley knew what would happen next, poor Pauline did not have a clue. She expected to go and find the glove and go on to enjoy herself at the dance with the added bonus of getting some records, not a bad night all in all. Unfortunately as we know this was not going to be the outcome of that fateful evening.

Brady asked Pauline to accompany him onto the right hand side of the A635 moor to an area known as Hollin Brown Knoll. Brady suggested to Hindley, she should park the van at another lay-by a little further up the road. He then said to Pauline let's get going and find this glove then we can get you back before your dance finishes, Hindley will join us when she has moved the van.

Hindley sat in the van while Brady and Pauline disappeared onto the moor.

Hindley later stated it was around half an hour before Brady returned to the Mini Van alone. He instructed Hindley to follow him to a secluded spot on the moor. He seemed pleased

Hindley followed Brady to the secluded spot. A horrendous image lay in front of her; the body of a once lively young 16 year old girl.

Pauline was lay on her back. Her clothes were in an untidy state which led Myra to believe Brady had raped the young girl. She was not dead at the time Hindley arrived at the scene, she was making a horrid stomach churning gurgling sound. Pauline died a few minutes later, her last moments would have seemed like an eternity, looking up the final faces she would see would be that of the most dangerous people she had ever met, the two people she thought she could trust.

Brady had killed Pauline by cutting her throat; he had cut her so deeply he had virtually decapitated her. He then left Hindley alone; she states she never looked at the body because it horrified her. She said the cut on Pauline's neck was so deep it surprised her because Brady had meant to strangle her. To avoid having to look at Pauline, Hindley says she looked at the outline of the rocks against the horizon, and three people died that night; Pauline, my soul and god. This statement of where she was looking would later lead Topping and his men to Pauline's burial site.

After what apparently felt like an eternity Brady returned saying he was having trouble locating the area in which he had previously placed the spade in a nearby gas line trench.

The spade had been bought purposely for the job of burying their victim that night, purchased from a hardware shop in Gorton. Hindley said that Brady's clothes were now a crimson colour and dripping with blood resulting from the virtual beheading of Pauline.

At this point Brady instructed Hindley to go and wait back at the van for him to ensure nobody could approach, while he finished his perfect murder by burying Pauline in a secluded area of Saddleworth Moor, a vast area Brady believed nobody would be able to locate the victim. Hindley stumbled across the moor land towards the road where the Mini Van was parked. When she approached the driver side door she realised why it had taken Brady so long to return to her when he was locating the spade. He had returned to the van which Hindley had left with the keys in and unlocked in case they needed to escape quickly. Brady had removed the keys from the ignition. Hindley sat in the driver's seat waiting for Brady to return.

Eventually Brady returned he was carrying the bloody knife he had used to end the young girls life and the dirty spade he had used to try and conceal his crime. He approached the Mini Van, got in the passenger side and wrapped the knife in a piece of newspaper he placed the spade in a bag ready to be cleaned at home so no evidence could lead back to the burial site. Brady then placed the spade into the back of the Mini van and the knife upon the dashboard.

However Brady's account of the murder of Pauline differs quite considerably to that of Hindley's.

Firstly Brady states he, Pauline and Myra all left the Mini Van together and walked up onto the moors in search for the lost glove.

Once all three were in the desired location he states 'not only did Hindley witness the rape and murder of Pauline she took a very active part in the rape of the young girl, he stated in a letter in 1990 that Hindley was so vigorous towards the young girl she had caused physical damage to the girls nose and forehead. He also alleged during the murder of Pauline he had hit Hindley because even though he knew that during the course of the evening he had dropped to the depths of depravity. Hindley had "dropped even further by taking the gold locket which belonged to Joan Reade and taunting the girl by saying you won't need this where you're going".

In Brady's book The Gates of Janus Brady writes 'it is human nature that if caught, the pupil will blame his master for his criminal conduct. But should the criminal enterprises succeed, I can assure you, from wide personal experience, that pupils zeal and devotion to criminal activities can outdo that of the master like that of a convert.'

Whichever way it occurred an innocent life was taken that night upon the bleak moors.

On the way to collect the Tiger cub Hindley said Brady made a comment about Pauline saying 'for a while when he was killing Pauline she struggled so much he thought he may have needed Myra's help'.

They arrived at the lay by where the Tiger cub was parked and as previously planned they dragged two long planks of wood out of the back of the Mini van position to be used as a makeshift ramp, to get the bike onto the van.

They drove home in silence reflecting on the evenings activities. Brady was the first to talk, he told Hindley had she shown any indication of wanting to back out she would have ended up in the grave he had dug for Pauline. Her reply was short; she said 'I know that'.

When they were eventually back on Gorton Lane, Hindley saw two figures walking towards them coming from the direction of Cornwall Street. The two figures were Joan and Paul Reade searching for Pauline, Hindley told Brady "that's her mother and brother". She turned the corner into Croft Street near Bannock Street and turned off. They took the Tiger Cub out of the back of the Mini Van and walked around the corner to Bannock Street. When they entered the house Brady took the knife and spade and locked them away in a cupboard ready to be cleaned of any evidence. Ian then reminded Hindley she was supposed to be helping Ben Boyce whose Mini Van she had borrowed to recover his broken down grocers van in nearby Abbey Hey. Brady said if she did not go then Ben would get suspicious because Hindley had promised him. Brady fastened up his over coat to cover his blood soaked clothes and ushered Hindley out of the door.

Back at the Reade household Joan and Amos were getting extremely worried.

Joan heard a noise outside and went out to investigate thinking it may have been Pauline, there was no sign of her but on the ground a few doors down was Pauline's glove, she was sure it wasn't there earlier when herself and Paul were out looking.

When Pauline still hadn't arrived home by midnight Joan and Amos called the police, they searched all night but she had simply vanished. There were speculations Pauline had runaway, no matter what people said the Reade's knew Pauline was not the kind of girl to do such a thing.

Back at the house Brady got on with what he called his 'disposal plan', it was now time to get rid of any evidence.

On Myra's return they started with the van, Hindley fetched a bucket of hot soapy water. Brady cleaned the van. He cleaned the exterior including the tyres. While Brady had been cleaning, he informed Hindley he had found four half crowns in Pauline's pocket and had spent them on the on Woodbine cigarettes and a crunchie bar for her. Back in the house they locked the door and closed the curtains and made sure Gran was asleep.

Once all the checks had been made to ensure they would not be disturbed they lay out sheets of plastic on the lounge floor where Brady sat and started cutting up his blood soaked clothes so they would burn quickly. He threw them into the fire in the lounge along with his shoes. He said the best way to dispose of evidence is to burn it.

Brady then attempted to dispose of the knife by snapping off the handle but this attempt failed so he just threw the knife into the fire. Lastly Hindley scrubbed out the cupboard where they had stored the knife and spade; she scrubbed it with hot soapy water to ensure all traces of evidence were gone.

Hindley said once the clean up was complete Brady produced a bottle of Drambuie to toast what he declared as the perfect murder. His ambition to commit the perfect murder was now a dream come true.

Hindley said he had asked how she felt about it and she replied 'I never in my wildest dreams imagined something like this could have happened and started to cry. He put his arm around me and clumsily kissed me on the cheek, telling me it was all over now, I'd learn to live with it and he would try to control his temper and not hit or hurt me. I was so relieved I clung to him, still crying and promised I'd do everything I could to cope with what had happened and do my best not to antagonise him, although I rarely did and he still hit and hurt me.

He stroked my hair—"I thought the merest touch would repel me, but in spite of what had happened this new tenderness touched me to the core of my heart and flooded it with all the love and emotions I'd felt for him for so long."

In Brady's book 'The Gates of Janus' he stated after the first murder a serial killer feels 'I'm no longer of your world-if, as you might suggest, I ever was.'

Joan and Amos posted a notice in the local paper the Manchester Evening News saying "please come home, we are heartbroken". When Hindley read the notice in the paper she said she broke down crying and Brady began to strangle her resulting in bruising to her neck.

Joan would leave her back door open every night hoping her daughter would return home. It would be 25 years later before they would learn exactly what had happened to her.

# EPISODE 8

'Sorrow is knowledge, those that know the most must mourn the deepest, the tree of knowledge is not the tree of life'.

**Lord Byron**

# John Kilbride

John Kilbride was aged 12 when he disappeared from Ashton under Lyne market on the 23rd November 1963.

John was born on the 15th May 1951 to parents Patrick and Sheila Kilbride. He was the eldest of the couple's children and was closely followed by 4 brothers Danny, Pat, Terry, Chris and two sisters Sheila and Maria.

They all lived together in a regular 3 bed-roomed house on Smallshaw Lane in Ashton.

John attended the local Catholic high school, St Damien's on Lee's Road in Ashton; he started there in the September 1962.

He was a happy outgoing well natured boy, and always happy to help others. He was a regular visitor to his Granny Doran who lived round the corner helping her with odd jobs that she was unable to do due to ill health.

John was a keen fan of the cinema attending most Saturdays when he could or would be in the stands at his local football club Ashton United. He was a regular face being such a big fan of the team.

The Kilbride's were regular worshippers at their local Catholic Church; St Christopher's where John and later his brother Danny were choir boys. John had a lovely singing voice which seemed to run in the family as most of his brothers were excellent singers especially the youngest Chris, who later in life could often be found propping up the bar in a local pub singing his rendition of Danny Boy.

John was also recognised by most people for the way he walked everywhere with his hands in his trouser pockets whistling all the time mostly the theme tune to the TV show z cars.

On the morning of the 23rd of November 1963, John left his family home early in the morning to go and help Granny Doran with his usual morning jobs. He returned home just before lunch and went out into the back garden to speak to his brother Danny who was tending to his birds in the home made aviary. Not long after, three of John's friends came to call for him as they were all going to Ashton cinema to watch a film together incidentally all the four boys together were called John. As he was about to leave the house he grabbed one of his favourite jackets that had been given to his granny for him from one of her friends, what made it extra special was his mum had sewn on football buttons for him.

When the lads arrived at the cinema they were informed they could not see the movie as they were not old enough. To see the movie they would need adult supervision. Somehow they managed to persuade a passing stranger to be responsible for them, and they got to see the movie of their choice 'The Mongols'.

The movie finished around 5pm and by this time the streets were becoming increasingly dark as the cold winter nights grew close. John and the other three lads did the usual teenager thing and messed about on the streets for a while.

They soon grew bored and decided to go and see if any of the market stall holders needed any help so they could earn a little extra money.

Little did John know he had missed his dad by 20 minutes. His dad had been down to the market buying a new pair of shoes.

John Kilbride and one of his friends John Ryan went to fetch a trolley from the station for one of the stall holders and in return they got sixpence each. John Ryan explained to John Kilbride that he was going for the bus home to which John replied he was going to stay a little longer.

He was last seen, sitting on a wall near the large bins eating a bag of broken biscuits which he had bought with his sixpence. Then supposedly he was approached by a smartly dressed couple. John was never seen again.

*The Secret Key To The Moors Murders*

Earlier that very same day, Hindley hired a White Ford Anglia from Warren's Auto's purposely for the job they had planned for the day. She collected the car and headed to Westmoreland Street to meet Brady. When she arrived he handed her a gift, a record by Gene Pitney, '24 hours from Tulsa'. Brady got in the Anglia and they set off to Leek in Staffordshire 35 miles away. They spent the morning at Roaches lock.

One the way home they stopped off in Huddersfield where Hindley put on a black wig held in place by a head scarf and entered a hardware store to buy the murder kit for that evening; it consisted of, a small kitchen knife, a length of cord and a shovel. She returned to the car and popped the newly bought items in the boot.

When they reached the outskirts of Manchester they drove around several cinemas to find one that was showing a film they had previously seen 'From Russia with love' in case they ever needed an alibi for that night. Before dropping Brady home she removed the wig and headscarf and placed them aside for later that afternoon. She dropped Brady off at home and returned to her house at Bannock Street.

AT 4pm Brady arrived at Bannock street looking forward to the night's planned events. The pair lined the back of the hire car with polythene sheeting placed the murder kit in the back along with a torch and a rifle. They left Gorton heading towards Ashton;

They discussed the plan for the evening: Hindley would wait in the car while Brady took his victim onto the moors, she would then drive down to Greenfield wait half an hour then return to their designated spot and flash her head lights 3 times, and she would wait for Brady to flash his torch 3 times in response.

Upon arrival at Ashton Market, Brady told Hindley he had spotted his victim, a young boy sat on a wall near the bins eating biscuits. They approached the young boy. It is said John willingly left the market with the couple.

On the way to the car Brady promised him a bottle of Sherry saying he had won on a raffle. John jumped into the passenger seat of the car and put on his belt. Hindley locked the doors and off they went.

After a few moments Brady declared to John that they would have to call at their house in Greenfield for the promised bottle of Sherry. John was not disturbed by this unplanned detour and carried on gazing out of the window.

As they neared Greenfield, Brady broke spoke with Hindley saying that maybe they should go up to the moors to look for the lost glove.

Once on the moors Hindley parked up as planned and Brady asked John if he would help by fetching the torch from the boot of the car, Brady already had his murder kit tucked snugly inside his pockets. The pair started walking onto the moors, Hindley watched them go and put into place the previously agreed plan.

Once she was back on the moors she parked in the planned location and flashed her headlight, Brady flashed back. He appeared carrying one of the boy's shoes, he threw everything into the boot and said he couldn't kill him with the knife it wasn't sharp enough so he had strangled him with the cord instead.

Peter Topping claimed Brady told him in one of their many interviews, after he had killed John he looked up at the sky and said "take that you bastard".

In Brady's book 'The Gates of Janus', Brady wrote "nothing less than challenging god or the indifferent universe will satisfy. A form of reversed hope by stopping me" . . . to be ignored is to be deprived of human dignity and meaning".

When the pair returned to Bannock Street they set about putting the disposal plan into place. They claimed they threw John's shoe in to the fire. They cleaned all the soil and trace evidence from the shovel and locked it in a cupboard with the rifle. Into the fire went Brady clothes and he supposedly snapped the handle from the blade of the knife and threw the handle into the fire, he disposed of the blade separately. We believe differently.

Back in Ashton, John had not arrived home. By 6pm Patrick and Sheila really began to worry as John was a boy never to stay out late. Danny was sent round to their cousins' house to see if he was there, he also had a look around the local streets but to no avail.

By 9pm Patrick and Sheila were going out of their minds with worry, Sheila went round to the boys aunts house to phone the police as they did not have one at home at the time.

At first light the next day a full scale search was put into place for John, searching in peoples shed's, attics, coal bunkers and basically anywhere a teenager could be hiding.

Danny, his younger brother did the reconstruction of Johns last known movements on Ashton market to try and jog people's memories.

It would be two years of unexplainable heartache for the family until they would know for certain of John's fate.

*The Secret Key To The Moors Murders*

The centre of the cross made with rope and Red Electric Flex

The Cross found buried in a Sheep Pen we found SOUTH

*Erica Gregory*

A 5ft Mile Stone to the right of this would of been Yorkshire.

Polythene and white wire ligature buried in
Sheep Pen under the cross

The Lion Head Rock.
Ulysses mentions the Lion Head Cliff

The Split Oak Tree area where the bones of two sheep were found buried at the base. Brady's Hells Door?

*The Secret Key To The Moors Murders*

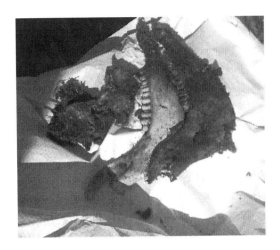

The Sheep bones were placed and buried at the base of the Oak Tree.

Tins and Glass Buried under a crag at the base of the hill near the sheep pen.

The symbol of an Esoteric Triangle on a pyramid shaped rock near to the shovel. is this a map?

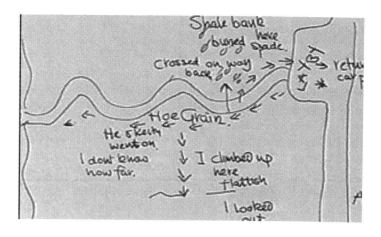

The crude map drawn for Myra. Our way in this shows the area we found the shovel Buried.

*The Secret Key To The Moors Murders*

The shovel. Buried in a shale bank by the steam. A grave digging shovel. Symbol of Hamlet, Shakespeare's play is mentioned in Ulysses.

The remains of a shoe that was wrapped in the wire ligature item has been burnt.

# EPISODE 9

## KEITH BENNETT

"If I had a flower for every time I thought of you . . . I could walk through my garden forever."

Alfred Lord Tennyson Poet.

---

Keith Bennett was a happy 12 year old boy when he disappeared on the 16th June 1964, four days after his 12th birthday.

He lived in a very busy family home at 29 Eston Street in Longsight with his mum Winnie, step-dad Jimmy Johnson and Keith's younger siblings, Alan, Margaret, Sylvia and step sister Susan who was extremely close to him and shared the same age.

Winnie had suffered extreme heartache several times over in her life, firstly she was scarred by the death of her sister, who had died at the age of 7, her dress had caught on fire in their childhood home, then later, the disappearance of her cherished son Keith.

Winnie and Keith's Dad separated when Keith was a young boy. Winnie married his step-dad in 1961. Keith became very close to his step-dad and began to call him dad.

The family was complete until that fateful night on the 16th June.

Winnie had arranged for Keith, Margaret and Alan to stay with her mum 65 year old Gertrude Bennett at her home on Morten Street. While she attended the 8pm session of bingo at St Aloysius school in Ardwick.

Alan and Margaret left their Eston Street home closely followed by Winnie and Keith. Winnie only being weeks away from having her 5th child was walking a little slower behind than usual. She wanted to ensure Keith crossed Stockport Road safely as he had broken his glasses the day before and his eye sight was poor without them. Winnie watched her son across the zebra crossing where he met up with two young girl's he knew from school and was trying to act tough around them, Winnie remembered being worried that he would hurt the girl's because of the way he was behaving.

Winnie continued on to bingo and Keith to his Gran's. When Keith approached the area of Upper Plymouth Grove he came across the two people who would ruin his family's life forever.

Earlier that day Brady and Hindley were making their own plan's for the evening ahead. Brady gave Hindley his latest gift Roy Orbison's 'It's Over' which is about mourning the loss of a loved one. It was early evening on a warm sunny day Hindley set out to collect Brady from Westmoreland Street, stopping on the way to pull on a black wig. Hindley arrived and Brady climbed into the back seat of the white mini traveller. They were about to put into practise the rehearsed plan, which would be, when Brady saw his victim he would knock on the glass to alert Hindley, she was to pull over and use the story of needing help moving some boxes. Once the victim was in the mini traveller they would drive to the Moors and park at the Shiny Brook lay by. (Supposedly)

Driving along Upper Plymouth Grove, Hindley spotted Keith and claims she already knew the young boy would be the one. Brady was knocked on the glass. It was then they put their plan into action.

Once they had reached the Shiny Brook lay by Brady and Keith left the mini van and started walking with Hindley following closely behind. Brady had his camera around his neck and Hindley a set of binoculars. They apparently walked beside a stream, crossing it several times keeping mainly kept to the right hand side; neither of them was carrying a shovel. Hindley remarked that Brady must have buried it previously.

Once they were quite a distance from the road Brady signalled for Hindley to stop. She climbed up on to a grassy plateau and looked through the binoculars at the horizon to keep watch for shepherds and hikers. Brady and Keith walked 25 to 30 yards into a ditch. Hindley says' that she was alone for about 30 or 40 minutes waiting for Brady to return. She recalled that at one point she thought somebody was approaching but it ended up being a sheep.

Brady came back carrying the spade, Hindley asked how he had killed the boy and he said he had sexually abused him and strangled him with a piece of string. He added that he had taken a picture which he showed her a few days later. She said there was blood on the body but she didn't look closely at the picture. Brady said he was going to dispose of it because it was blurry. Hindley did state that Keith was lay on his back with his trousers down and she could not tell on the picture whether or not he was alive or dead.

They walked together back down the stream bed; Brady said he was going to bury the shovel into a shale bank on the way back. Myra later stated that Keith had gone 'like a lamb to the slaughter'.

Back at home in Gorton, they began to put Brady's disposal plan into practice. He counted all the button's on their clothes as they had done previously and they burnt their shoes, Myra's had to be burnt as well as she had been stood with Brady on the shale bank when he buried the shovel.

He also cut up his clothes and put them in the fire along with the cord used to end young Keith's life.

It wasn't till the next morning when Gertrude Bennett brought Alan and Margaret home, they realised Keith was missing.

When Keith had not turned up at her house the previous night, she presumed he had decided to stay at home. In those days the family did not have a telephone so they could not phone each other to check if they had arrived.

Winnie went to the police to report her son as a missing person.

The search began for Keith and the police focused their search on railway lines as he had a love of trains and railways and could often be found by the tracks.

The search continued and on June 19th The Manchester Evening News ran an article on page 17 under the headline 'tracker dogs join hunt for lost boy'. Posters were put up showing a picture of Keith's smiling face with the description of the clothes he was wearing when he vanished and his physical description; 12 years old, 4ft 8inches, proportionate build, blue eyes, fair hair, very short sighted (not wearing glasses) wearing white leather jacket, zip fastener with pockets each side, blue jeans, striped lilac t-shirt and black plastic shoes.

Unlike Sheila Kilbride and Ann West, Winnie would have a very long wait to find out what had happened to her son

# EPISODE 10

## LESLEY-ANN DOWNEY

"I miss you like the sun misses the flower. Like the sun misses the flower in the depths of winter".

Quote a Knights Tale 2001

---

Lesley Ann Downey was 10 years old when she disappeared on the 26th December 1964.

Lesley Ann was a happy shy little girl who had the sweetest look of a porcelain doll. She lived at 25 Charnley Walk, Ancoats with her mum Ann, step dad Alan and her three brothers Terry aged fourteen, Thomas eight and Brett four. Lesley enjoyed dancing and singing like most young girls of her age and had even attended a dance not long before her disappearance with her elder brother Terry.

Lesley attended school at Trinity Methodist Church's girl's Guidry, where she was liked by everyone and had a few close friends.

The fair had arrived in town and Lesley was excited to be going on Boxing Day. Terry had already been to the fair with his friends where he won a white plastic necklace and matching bracelet. He sneaked into Lesley's room and placed them on her dressing table for her to see the next morning. When she woke the next morning she saw Terry's gift. She put them on and then ran to find him to give him a hug.

Every time Lesley's mum opened the kitchen window the music from the fair would carry through the flat to an excited little Lesley who couldn't wait to go that afternoon. Ann was trying to preoccupy her daughter by saying she would help her make some clothes for her dolls when she got back from the fair on the new sewing machine she had received the day before as a Christmas gift. Just before 4pm a very eager, Lesley threw on her coat and together with her brother Tommy said goodbye to their parents and left the flat to call at Mrs Clarkes downstairs. Mrs Clarke had planned to go to the fair for an hour with her three children, Lesley's friend Linda, and her younger brother and sister, Roy and Ann.

However on arrival Mrs Clarke declared herself to be too tired to escort the children to the fair, unfazed by this the five of them set off. They had all promised to be back by 5 o' clock.

The kids had a great time at the fair and by 5 o' clock had empty pockets to show for it, they decided to start making their way home but half way up Iron Street passing the old gasworks Lesley declared I'm going back and shot off back towards the fair while the other four carried on home.

A witness later recalled he saw Lesley stood memorized by the Dodgem cars; it was at this point around 6pm. He remembered racing passed her to go on a ride called cyclone, one of the rides Lesley had been on earlier that afternoon. He declared that was the last he saw of her.

Lesley was startled by a woman stood by her who had dropped her groceries.

Earlier in Hattersley, Hindley and Brady were having a very different start to their day.

It was Hindley's uncle Jims birthday and around lunch time she would be taking Granny Maybury to her son's home in Dukinfield so she could spend the day with him. The pair had already prepared some of what needed doing by removing a suitcase full of incriminating evidence from Hindley's room to its other storage space at the left luggage at Manchester's Central Station. Again, Brady gave Hindley a gift, a record, "Girl Don't Come" by Sandi Shaw.

Myra left at lunch time with granny and headed to Dukinfield whilst Brady stayed behind to prepare Hindley's bedroom for his next evil sick, twisted game.

He set up his camera and lights and placed the reel to reel tape recorder under the bed. Hindley returned and informed Brady that granny did not need to be collected until 9:30 that night.

It was late afternoon when they started to put their plan into action; they drove to a nearby supermarket to do some shopping especially for the plan and loaded it carelessly into two cardboard boxes. They returned to the car and placed the boxes into the boot. Hindley got out her black wig and head scarf and placed it on her head.

The pair then headed to the fair. They parked the car on a nearby side street away from the eyes of any nearby people.

They approached the fair, arms laden with boxes. They stood for a good 5 minutes in the dark shadows of the dodgems watching a little girl enthralled with the lights. When they were sure she was alone they made their move. They purposely made groceries spill out of the clumsily packed boxes next to Lesley Ann which grabbed her attention. She bent down to help. Hindley then smiled at her and asked if she would help them carry the boxes back to the car. They offered Lesley a reward; she was probably hoping it would be a few pence so she could go on a few more rides. She jumped at the chance and followed the couple to where the car was parked. Once at the car, Hindley asked Lesley if she would help unload the boxes back at their house and thinking of the reward and maybe the chance to go on some more rides, she quickly agreed and jumped into the passenger seat where she had boxes piles around her to keep her from view. Back at Wardlebrook Avenue, Hindley asked Lesley to take the boxes upstairs, unbeknown to her Brady was waiting for her. Hindley was supposed to be joining them straight away, but had to deal with the dogs which had escaped into the hallway.

As Hindley was locking the dogs in the kitchen, she claims she heard Lesley scream because Brady was trying to undress her. We don't have to believe either of their accounts as to what happened for the next few moments as it was captured on tape; the transcript can be found widely on the internet.

After Brady had finished whatever he was doing while the tape was running which many people have their own opinions on, Brady opened the tripod and set up the camera, he then unplugged the tape recorder to plug in his photography lights as there was only a single plug socket in the room. The pair then forced the young girl to undress and one of them tied a scarf around the lower half of her face, it was so tight that it would have been impossible for her to breathe. Brady then commenced to take 9 very disturbing pictures of Lesley in several different poses.

Hindley stated that she had been sent by Brady to run a bath for Lesley to remove any incriminating evidence from the body. She said it was during this time that Brady raped and murdered young Lesley.

Apparently after 20 minutes she had to re-run the bath as the water was cold. Many people believe it was indeed Hindley that killed Lesley, in her statement about re running the water because it was cold, why would she be concerned about the water temperature if she knew Lesley would be dead when entering the bath? She wasn't concerned that her boyfriend was raping and killing a poor innocent 10 year old, but the waters temperature had to be right. In our opinion she's was being too obvious in trying to remove herself from the actual murder as she did with Pauline. She goes on to say she went into the bedroom and saw Lesley lay on the bed with a strangulation mark around her neck and blood down her legs and on the sheet below. Brady bathed poor Lesley to remove any evidence then lay her back on the bed for the scarf to be removed. As with Pauline, Brady stated that it was indeed Hindley that killed Lesley Ann and that she used a 2 foot length of silk cord that she then used to toy with in public, knowing what it had been secretly used for. Brady never changed the accounts of the murders of the boys, only the girls.

So this again makes us believe the girls were Hindley's and the boys Brady's. They went to bury Lesley's body that night, but due to bad weather conditions they could not access Saddleworth moor. They drove to Dukinfield to tell Uncle Jim she couldn't take granny home that night and quickly darted off.

They took Lesley's body back into the house in Hattersley and placed her in Hindley's room for the night. Hindley claimed she never slept in there again. We know this isn't true as she and her sister Maureen spent many a night cuddled up on the single bed in that room while David Smith was becoming Brady's student.

Early the next morning they returned to the car to attempt to go and bury Lesley with the other lost souls on Saddleworth Moor.

Hindley parked at the usual spot at Hollin Brown Knoll and as it had happened 3 times before, off Brady went with the young child.

Back in Ancoats the previous night, when Anne had learnt that Lesley hadn't returned with the others from the fair, herself and Alan her husband threw on their coats, shouted to Terry to look after his younger brothers, they ran to the fairground and could not find poor Lesley.

All evening they were backwards and forwards between the flat and the fair, stopping to see if she was at Mrs Clarks house, and when they learnt she wasn't, Ann shouted at Mrs Clarke for bailing out on the children. They searched all night and when they realized they weren't going to find her, they reported her missing to the police. It would be 10 months before they finally knew what had happened to their sweet angelic little angel.

# EPISODE 11

"However it came about, and I cannot pretend to explain it, there was no doubt that Willie Hughes suddenly became to me a mere myth, an idle dream, the boyish fancy of a young man who, like most ardent spirits, was more anxious to convince others than to be himself convinced."
—Oscar Wilde . . . The Portrait of Mr W.H.

## Edward Evans.

---

Edward Evans turned 17 in the summer of 1965, tall and slim, with light brown hair and an engaging smile; he lived with his parents Edith and John and his brother Allan and sister Edith. They lived at 55 Addison Street Ardwick Greater Manchester. The following year the estate like many at the time was going to be demolished.

The Evan's family were extremely close and private both before and after Edwards's demise.

Edward had a job as a junior machine operative at associated electrical industries LTD on the Trafford Park industrial estate. Edwards's job was high paid at the time and he was bringing in more money than his father who worked as a lift attendant.

Edward was the kind of lad who lived by the motto 'work hard and play hard', after a long day at work he would enjoy going out with his friends, having a drink or watching his favourite football team Manchester United play. He was often a face seen in the stands at Old Trafford the teams home ground.

His close friend Jeff Grimsdale, described him as a happy go lucky kind of lad with many friends and a very sociable lad who always had a group of friends around him. Whenever his parents started to lecture him about how worried they were regarding his nights out partying he would give them his award winning smile and tell them 'I can handle any trouble'.

On that fateful day Wednesday 6th October 1965 that quote would become untrue.

On that evening Edward arrived home early from work to get ready for a night out watching Manchester United vs. Helsinki, He ate his tea and went upstairs to change. Just after 6pm Edward said goodbye to his mum, neither of them realised that would be the last time he would say those words. His mother Edith recalls 'Edward went out between 6 and 6.30, "I didn't see him alive again'.

Edward's friend who was supposed to meet him in Aunt's bar on Oxford Road in Manchester did not realise the arrangements they had made to meet was for definite, as they had not confirmed the details. Edward was sat in the bar at 7.30pm alone and was talking to the landlord whilst waiting for his friend.

George Smith the landlord recalled 'it was very unusual for him to come in on his own'. Edward finished his drink and when he realised his friend was not coming he bid George a good night and walked out of the bar.

Between 10-10.30pm the match had finished and Edward decided to call at Manchester's Central Station for a drink, when he got there he found the buffet bar was closed, he went to stand at the milk vending machine while deciding what to do next.

Earlier in Manchester Brady and Hindley sat eating breakfast together, what they didn't realise was it would be for the last time.

Brady gave Hindley yet another gift to mark the upcoming murder for that evening, this was Joan Baez's single 'It's over now baby blue'. The pair went to work as usual and finished as usual, nothing they did would lead people to suspect what was going to happen that evening. In preparation for the evening's events Brady had already taken any damming evidence out of their home and placed it in the left luggage at Manchester's Central Station.

The suitcase also contained the book's Brady had asked David Smith to return to him in preparation for 'the bank job' they planned for on the Saturday. The parcel of book's that were returned :—Mein kampf; Tropic of Cancer, Kiss of the Whip, The Life and Ideals of the Marquis De Sade, Justine, Orgies of Torture and Brutality and The Perfumed Garden. Most of these books had been banned at one time or another and could only be purchased from specialty bookshops.

Brady and Hindley were sat at home at 16 Wardle Brook Avenue, at 8pm there was a knock on the door Brady opened it to a worried David Smith, Brady let him in and Dave handed him a letter he had received from Mr Johnson the rent man. The letter read; 'Mr Smith, I want £14,12s,6 D at the town hall on Saturday or I shall take legal proceedings. Mr Page is doing his job and if that dog is not out of the building by tonight I shall have you evicted". If there are any more complaints of Teddy boys and noise, I shall take further action. Brady shrugged the letter off asking what Dave thought he could do about it. Dave explained that the money wasn't a problem he could borrow that from his dad, it was the thought of losing another dog having had to have one put to sleep previously. Brady again shrugged it off and hurried Dave out of the house saying he and Hindley were going out. Hindley was putting her finishing touches to her make-up, she was wearing a Leopard Print dress. She grabbed the car keys and they both made their way to the car.

They drove the short distance to Manchester Central Station. Once there Hindley refused to pay the parking fees so she stopped on yellow lines to wait while Brady went in.

Hindley jumped at a loud knocking on her driver's window, it was a police officer, she explained she was just waiting for her boyfriend who had nipped to the buffet, the officer said if she was still there on his return round he would have to book her and off he went.

Brady approached the buffet. In his statement Brady said 'Evan's was standing at a milk vending machine. I know Evan's; I had met him on several occasions previously, as I went to try the (buffet) door, he said it was closed, but I tried the door anyway. Then we got into conservation. He kept saying there was no place to get a drink . . . I invited him back to the car'. Brady had invited Edward back to the house in Hattersley for a drink and at the car he introduced Edward to Hindley as his sister.

They arrived back at the house on Wardle Brook Avenue. Brady asked Hindley to call on David Smith.

Just after 11pm David and Maureen Smith were woken by their intercom. Maureen got up to answer while David got dressed. It was Myra and she buzzed her in.

David later stated that she must of accompanied Brady and Edward into 16 Wardle Brook Avenue because when he had seen her earlier that evening she had on a Leopard Print dress and her make-up and hair was perfect, but when she arrived in their flat at Underwood Court her hair was a mess, her make-up smudged and she had an old jumper on and an old skirt with the hem hanging down and scruffy pump's on.

When Maureen later testified in court she stated; 'she said she wanted to give me a message to give to my mother, to tell her she would see her at the weekend and she could not get up there before . . . I asked her why she had come round so late and she said it was because she had forgotten earlier on and she had just remembered.

I asked her why she had not got the car and she said because she had locked it up . . . She asked if David would he walk her round to Wardle Brook Avenue because all the lights were out . . . David said he would, and he got ready'. David grabbed his stick and walked Hindley home, as they approached the house Hindley told David that Brady had some Miniature Bottles for him and he may as well collect them while he was there. Hindley told David to wait across the road and wait for the lights to flash on and off.

David told the court later on 'I did not think this was unusual because I have had to do this before whilst she, Myra, went in to see if Ian would have me in. He's a very temperamental sort of fellow. I waited across the road as Myra told me and then the landing light flickered twice, so I walked up and knocked on the front door.

Ian opened the door and he said in a very loud voice for him, he normally speaks soft, 'do you want those miniatures?' I nodded my head to show 'yes' and he led me in to the kitchen, which is directly opposite the front door and he gave me three miniature bottles of spirits and said; 'do you want the rest'.

'When I first walked into the house, the door to the living room—which was on my right, standing at the front door—was closed. After he put the three bottles down in the kitchen, Ian went in to the living room and I waited in the kitchen. I waited about a minute or two, then suddenly I heard a hell of a scream; it sounded like a woman, really high-pitched. Then the screams carried on, one after another, really loud. Then I heard Myra shout, 'Dave, help him', very loud . . .

When I ran in, I just stood inside the living room and I saw a young lad, about 17 years old . . . he was laying his head and shoulders on the couch, and his legs were on the floor. He was facing upwards. Ian was standing over him, facing him, with his legs on either side of the young lad's legs. The lad was still screaming, he did not look injured then, but there was only a small television light on, the big light was off. Ian had a hatchet in his hands, I think it was his right hand, it was his right hand, he was holding it above his head, and then he hit the lad on the left side of his head with the hatchet, I heard the blow, it was a terrible hard blow, it sounded horrible. The young lad was still screaming, and the lad half-fell and half-wiggled of the couch onto the floor onto his stomach. He was still screaming, Ian went after him and stood over him and kept hacking away at the young lad with the hatchet, but it was a lot, about the head, about the neck, you know that region, the shoulders and that . . . I felt my stomach turn when I saw what Ian did, and some sick came up and then it went down again. I could not move, when he, Ian, that is, was hacking at the lad, they got close to me and one of the blows Ian did at the lad grazed my right leg. I remember Ian was swinging about with the hatchet and one blow grazed the top of Myra's head . . . After Ian stopped hitting the lad, he was lying on his face, with his feet next to the door. I could hear a gurgling noise in the lad's throat . . . Ian got a cover of one of the chairs and wrapped it around the lad's head. There was blood all over the place on the walls, fireplace, everywhere . . .

'Ian never spoke a word all this time, and he got a cord, I think it was electric wire, I don't know where he got it from and he wrapped it round the lad's neck, one end of the cord in one hand and one end in the other and then he crossed the cord and pulled and kept pulling until the gurgling stopped in the lad's throat. All the time Ian was doing this, strangling the lad, Ian was swearing, 'you dirty bastard'. He kept saying that over and over again. Myra was still there all this time, just looking. Then Ian looked up at Myra and said something like: it's done, it's the messiest yet, it normally only takes one blow'.

I suddenly became very calm, knowing I could not put a foot wrong if I was to survive. I knew I had to show no emotion, no bad reaction to what he had done or I would not be going home, It frightened me to think I was even capable of that'. David turned to look at Hindley; she was starring at a silent Brady who lit himself a cigarette. Brady wiped his hands on a piece of material, switched the main light on and told Hindley to go in to the kitchen and get a mop and bucket, a bowl of soapy water and some rags.

David told the court 'Myra did that and Ian turned to me and said, 'your sticks a bit wet' and he grinned at me. The stick he meant was a stick I had taken with me when I went with Myra from our place, it is like a walking stick and the only thing I could think is that when I rushed in to the living-room at first I had dropped it, because it was lying on the floor near the young lad . . ." Then Myra came in with the bowls of water and that, she did not appear upset, she had just stepped over the young lad's body and placed the bowls of soapy water on the floor".

# EPISODE 12

# Important dates and connections

Not only do we have the actual links between James Joyce and Ian Brady's ideas, and Myra Hindley, Nora Joyce and the character Molly Bloom from Ulysses, we also have many key dates regarding other writings linking to James Joyce's that can also be connected. Music is a major part in all Joyce's work. Something Brady and Hindley used as a code, with the giving of Records.

**Pauline Reade 12th July 1963**
**Romanticism**

Firstly let's start with Piero Coppola (11th October 1988-17th March 1971), was an Italian conductor/Pianist . . . of La Vorx De Son Mattre, the French branch of the gramophone company.

In 1924 he was asked by Sylvia Beach to make a recording of James Joyce. Piero Coppola also recorded Ravels Bolero, Brady and Hindley played this music loudly from their house on the day of Pauline Reade's murder. Again here we have a connection to the Shakespeare and co bookshop in Paris during the 1920s.

James Joyce also wrote many letters that have been published, one of these was on the 12th July, and this date is significant as Pauline Reade was murdered on this day. The letter from Joyce to his future wife Nora, after a first date and the beginning of their relationship uses the glove as a symbol.

"Your glove lay beside me all night . . . Unbuttoned . . . but otherwise conducted itself properly". I was beginning to see that Ian Brady was now a symbolist, many serial killers leave items to mark areas they have touched, is this now what we are seeing.

Pauline's white glove was found by her mother a few hours after Pauline had disappeared outside a neighbour's house, she had insisted it hadn't been there earlier that night when she had been out looking for Pauline. According to the time of evening, the glove was found it matches the same time that Hindley and Brady stated they were back from the moors. Also nobody knew why the pair had used the lost glove idea to entice the children up to the moors, this now seems like Myra's diaries and letters may have been part of a sick parlour game, involving really what these comments were meaning. Nobody had a clue except Ian Brady just what these were really saying.

The Shakespeare pub was not far from Pauline's home. So here we have the importance of a date, Pauline's glove, the music of Ravels Bolero and Shakespeare all in one of the Children's story. Was this the beginning of Brady's plans? Or had this already started earlier and was just a continuation of other murders in another area of Manchester. Brady giving Hindley the music from the film 'The legions last patrol', a film they watched together was also now coming to us as a symbol. They were known to whistle to each other, the music from this film, was this a sick coded message? The film the Legions last patrol, when looked into, starred an actress by the name of Dorian Gray. Dorian Gray is a gothic book written by Oscar Wilde. Oscar Wilde's work is also mentioned in James Joyce's work. The story about a portrait painting, the painting ages whilst the owner stays youthful. What we find is 'The Portrait of an Artist as a young man' written by James Joyce, this book which was written before Ulysses and seems to be the next book used for ideas.

## John Kilbride 23rd November 1963.
Dark Romanticism Gothic

There are several links here that we find have links with John Kilbride's disappearance.

James Joyce received a letter from HG Wells on this date. H G Welles, a science fiction writer whose work has influenced many, from film to pulp fiction magazines. Including The Day of the Triffids also watched with the Legions last Patrol as a double bill.

The name Kilbride appears in the book of Ulysses as an engine driver. If we now include the second book written by James Joyce a Portrait of an Artist, the book is the life of young Stephen Dedalus growing up.

Music given by Brady to Hindley for the start of this story is, 24 hours from Tulsa by Gene Pitney. Gene Pitney is a link to the Greenwich Village folk and Art scene in the USA. Researching the record revealed this. University of Tulsa 1963 begins the very first James Joyce Quarterly, which is a section all about the life and works of James Joyce from books, music and all his letters. They can be bought from the USA.

We can now link in the note book which Brady had written; this gave the police the indication that John Kilbride may have been one of their victims.

Not only did it contain John Kilbride's name but it also contained names of various actors. These names all seem to link to Gothic or science fiction films. Alec Guinness appeared in a film called 'The man in a white suit', an Ealing comedy with the theme of a mad scientist. Another Robert Urquhart appeared in Frankenstein. So the theme of dark Romanticism comes in here. Wuthering heights, Percy Shelley and the Byronic heroes came from Lord Byron.

The Green tapes found in the suitcases at the train station, which Brady himself had recorded, contained a clip from The Goons. The Goons were a comedy act which included Peter Sellers and Spike Milligan.

Lord Byron wrote a poem called Childe Harolde's pilgrimage; again found during re-search of the shows by the Goons we discovered that one of the episodes was titled Childe Harolde's pilgrimage.

If correct the tapes are a code to all four children on the Moors.

The one we found dated to the 23rd November is 'The Canal'. Ian Brady stated that a knife used on John Kilbride, was thrown into a canal after the murder.

Because we are saying that ideas have come from James Joyce's life and works, we now also think that using the word GREEN before the tapes was Brady's way of connecting Ireland.

We have a possible canal for the knife. In Ashton there is canal next to the Cavendish Mill.

The name of the Mill connects to a murder by a man called Joe Brady. He was a member of the political group called 'The Invincible's'. Joe Brady was responsible for the murder of two politicians, one a Lord Cavendish, who met in a park in Dublin.

Was the knife representing this murder? Again, mentioned in James Joyce's work. The Cavendish Mill, maybe a symbol?

One of John Kilbride's shoes was missing when his body was discovered, again a symbol.

Shoes were left in a suitcase found in the West area of the Saddleworth Moor. What this represents is not clear.

The missing shoe we believe has been found by us at the grave of Michael Higgins, Myra's young friend who drowned.

When Hindley was interviewed by Peter Topping about what was used to strangle John, she stated it was a white shoe lace like the one you would find in a white plimsoll. She also stated that she saw Brady putting the lace into the boot of the car after the murder. The mention of a white plimsolls and laces are mentioned in Ulysses as a murder weapon.

We find at the end of 'A Portrait of an Artist as a Young man' is that on the 15th June, Stephen Dedalus breaks his glasses. This is how the book ends to make way for the next book which is Ulysses.

Keith Bennett also broke his glasses on this date. Was this a coincidence? We believe that it is more than a possibility that Brady and Hindley were involved in that incident, and that getting to know and grooming children would have been quite easy to do.

16th June 1964. using important dates as part of Brady's Plans, on this date the 16th it is marking two. James Joyce's brother Stanislaus Joyce died. This also is the day acted out by many every year known as Bloomsday.

Ulysses Bloomsday, acted out in the South area of Dublin at Ringsend Park and environs.

Ian Brady gives Myra Hindley the record "It's over" by Roy Orbison. Roy Orbison is known as the voice of Greenwich Village.

If we are right to the links to Joyce, then we may also be right about the 16th June being in the South area of the moors at Greenfield. Keith Bennett's glasses were broken on the 15th June. So is the next day marked with the murder of Keith Bennett?

We are still searching for Keith or any other victims, while we write the book, we are hoping that one day soon we will be able to help find him and bring him home for a Christian burial with his beloved mother Winnie.

We are working in the area and have found many symbols.

The items found up to date are in the timeline in the WPG introduction.

The symbols we can also link in the mythology of the Greek story of Ulysses and Joyce's book. In the chapter Cyclops it ends with the saying 'like a shot of a shovel'. We have also found in this chapter, a mention of a boxing match between two characters. Keogh (Dublin's lamb), and Bennett. KB?

Myra would also quote that Keith was taken "like a lamb to the slaughter", the part of the moor we are searching contains areas known as Lamb Knoll and Lamb stones.

We have found many other items in that area which link to the writings of Joyce.

Two sheep were found sacrificed by a split Oak tree on a plateau area high up from the stream bed.

In Ulysses the Greek Myth, Ulysses is told to sacrifice two sheep to the underworld.

In the area there are many crags and cave like holes, also a large rock which resembles a Lions Head.

In Ulysses a witch called Circe lives in caves, the witch gives Ulysses poison to drink before the entrance to hell.

We have found in the area a drinking glass with a lid and many broken tins, buried under a crag, again down by the stream bed below the area of the sheep, these are all dated to the right period. The glass itself could be to symbolise the same as the story.

A lion's head cliff is also mentioned in Ulysses as part of the Circe chapter. This states that a person wrapped as a mummy is rolled down to the water below.

That area we are sure is far more likely for a victim to be buried than other areas of the moors. The items we have found all connect if the story of Ulysses was included in the murder plan for the 16th June.

Again we seem to have far too many coincidences in one place. The only reason being that these had been placed by someone for the very reason we are trying to explain.

The post-mortem cut sheep bones have been dated to the right age for 1962-67.

An item we uncovered on the 5th May 2013, is a crudely made cross entwined with red electrical flex and rope, this was discovered buried in a sheep pen near to the split oak tree. The pen is still being excavated as we finish the book.

We found an interesting fact, an Archaeologist by the name of Heinrich Schliemann, a hero of Joyce's, discovered Troy by reading poetry and writings.

He lent weight to the idea that Homers Iliad and Virgil's Aeneid reflect actual historical events. Schliemann discovered a grave circle of bodies through an area called the lions gate.

Joyce quoted that if Dublin should fall Schliemann would be the one to rediscover it.

Schliemann a German, who moved to Kaliningrad Russia, discovered some of the most important treasures in Greek history.

These are now on display in Russia. We believe that Brady would have been interested in him and his findings, especially because his work was based on ideas from poetry and literature.

Brady was well known for visiting museums, Art galleries and public libraries.

Here taken from a newspaper report, regarding a letter he sent, He writes about his visits to Glasgow with Hindley, Brady talks as if they were a normal couple enjoying a romantic break away, popping into art galleries and cinemas and drinking in posh clubs.

In a letter dated in April 2010 Brady advised another prisoner how to spend his time on release from prison, he recommended retracing the steps that he and Hindley took in Glasgow on their final visit.

Brady writes 'why not visit the museum and art gallery across from the Kelvin Hall?

## Lesley ANN Downey 26th December 1964
## Medievalism.

Schliemann died on 26th December, so if this was a man Brady was interested in, then this could be a significant date to Lesley Ann's disappearance.

We believe that she is connected to the medievalism, and again Art Films connected to Surrealism.

One film from the period of the 1920s is a film made by the Surrealist Artist Salvador Dali and film director Luis Bunuel. The film 'Un Chien Andalou' made in 1929, this visual Art film depicts symbolism and surrealism in a graphic and very strange way.

This film reminded us of some of the things that were found with the body of Lesley-Ann.

There is a scene where clothes are laid out at the foot of a bed, and a hand is cut off and carried in a box.

These are things which Ian Brady may have done, to symbolise his own Art. Was he influenced by ideas from film and others work?

We find that Chaucer's Canterbury Tales was also used as a code for Lesley Ann both outside and inside prison.

The Canterbury Tales is a book based on the ideas of the Medieval Knights. And the Teutonic Knights of the East. (Again a connection to The Rosicrucian and Freemason religion. A circle of crosses found in the area would be a symbol to the Knights of the Round Table).

A quote from the book states to 'Die in Bondage and Durance'. The book is also part of the Christmas period, where Christmas fairs and dinner parties are mentioned.

The music given to Hindley from Brady was Sandi Shaw's 'Girl don't come' which has the Greenwich Village connection again.

Brady and Hindley often spoke about trips to the cinemas.

Art films seemed to be of interest mainly to Brady. Two of the films we know for certain that Brady had watched were 'Devil Doll' this is said to have been watched around the time of Keith's murder, and the other one which is found in Brady's own book 'The Gates of Janus' is the Seventh Seal.

The Seventh seal (Swedish Det Sjunde Inseglet) is a 1957 Swedish film written and directed by Ingmar Bergman.

Set in Sweden during the Black Death, it tells of the journey of a medieval Knight (Max Von Sydow) and a game of chess he plays with the personification of death

(Bengi Ekerot), who has come to take his life. Bergman developed the film from his own play Wood Painting.

The title refers to a passage from the Book Of Revelation, used both at the very beginning of the film and again towards the end, beginning with the words 'and when the lamb has opened the Seventh Seal, there was silence in heaven about the space of half an hour'. Here the motif of silence refers to the 'silence of god' which is a major theme of the film.

Janus Films is a film distribution company; the distributor is credited with introducing numerous films, now considered masterpieces of world cinema, to American audiences.

These include the films of Michelangelo Antonio, Sergei Eisenstein, Ingmar Bergman, Federico Fellini and other worldwide directors.

Ingmar Bergman's The Seventh seal (1957) was the film responsible for the company's initial growth. Janus has a close relationship with The Criterion Collection regarding the release of its films on DVD and is still an active theatrical distributor.

The company's name and logo come from Janus the two faced roman god.

Janus films were founded in 1956 by Bryant Haliday and Cyrus Harvey Jr, in the historic Brattle Theatre, a Harvard square landmark in Cambridge Massachusetts.

Prior to the conception of Janus, Haliday and Harvey began screening both foreign and American films at the Brattle and proceeded to regularly fill the 300 seat venue. Having purchased the theatre, Haliday together with Harvey converted the Brattle into a popular movie house for showing Art films.

What we seem to have again is the importance of Art as part of the plans for the killings.

The Gates of Janus as a book title we now believe is telling us this also.

The Devil Doll film they watched is also part of the Janus films production.

The film I believe was part of the Edward Evans murder La Dolce Vita is also part of the Art film. Federico Fellini: La Dolce Vita.

This was one of the books left with Edwards's body.

Using Film as well as Music, and Photographs as part of the realism of the stories they brought to life.

I do know Ian Brady has sent many clues to people whom he writes to, music and themes from movies. These are cryptic messages that many have not realised. He has sent lists of Music from films, which link to surrealism, and stating that he was acting something out. One of the films I do know of was Groundhog Day, many will think this is a strange one, but what I have connected from this is.

GROUNDHOG DAY IS THE 2ND FEBRUARY, as I was already researching James Joyce's work and have Ulysses for the 16th June murder, I found this:-

James Joyce's Birthday 2nd February and Ulysses was also published on the 2nd February.

I looked into others mentioned on the lists and have come up with connections to his book 'The Gates of Janus' and also Ulysses.

These lists were not sent to me but to others Brady has written to in the past 10 years.

Going back to Lesley Ann and the period of Christmas, we also find connections to James Joyce.

Christmas is the time Joyce remembers as the worst time of his life. At home there were always arguments, at their table his father would bring up politics and one man especially a man called Charles Parnell.

Charles Stewart Parnell (born 27th June 1846—died 6th October 1891) was an Irish landlord, nationalist political leader and a land reform agitator, and the founder and leader of the Irish Parliamentary Party.

He was a hero of Joyce and appears in Finnegan's Wake as the character HCE.

Moving away from the Moors, We now feel Brady was now taking a turn towards a new story to act out, the book of Finnegan's Wake after the death of Lesley Ann Downey.

He was turning towards the political side of Joyce's work.

We bring in Joe Brady again here . . . . A character we feel Brady himself acted out along with the others for each story he created.

We now have the political link to Finnegan's Wake. There is a link to a group called the Invincibles, a group that was lead by a man called Joe Brady. He was hanged for the murder of two politicians in the Dublin's Phoenix Park. Joe Brady was brought up as a stonemason.

May 15th 1883 London Times recalled of the by then hanged man, 'of herculean strength, his occupation was developing the strength of the muscles in his arms, which told such terrible effect when he drove the knife into the bodies of the victims.

## Ballad of Joe Brady

I am a bold undaunted youth; Joe Brady is my name,
From the chapel of North Anne Street one Sunday as I came,
All to my surprise who should I espy but Moreno and Cockade;
Says one unto the other: "Here comes our Fenian blade".
I did not know the reason why they ordered me to stand,
I did not know the reason why they gave me such a command.
But when I saw James Carey there, I knew I was betrayed.
I'll face death before dishonour and die a Fenian blade.
They marched me up North Anne Street without the least delay,

The people passed me on the path, it filled them with dismay.
My sister cried, "I see you Joe, if old Mallon gives me lave,
Keep up your heart for Ireland like a true-born Fenian Blade.
It happened in the Phoenix Park all in the month of May,
Lord Cavendish and Burke came out for to see the polo play.
James Carey gave the signal and his handkerchief he waved,
Then he gave full information against our Fenian blades.
It was in Kilmainham Prison the Invincibles were hung.
Mrs Kelly she stood there all in mourning for her son.
She threw back her shawl and said to all:
"Though he fills a lime-pit grave,

Joe Brady, infamous in Ireland around the turn of the century and makes a small appearance in the referential soup of James Joyce's Ulysses for animal spirits of a different sort; a conversation about his hanging provides the departure point for a Joycean meander into the phenomenon of scaffold priapism. Death erection also mentioned all through the book 'Justine' by the Marquis De Sade. Another one of Ian Brady's favourite books!

Another Irish man here who became a hero was Brady's getaway driver James 'skin the goat' Fitzharris, who became a national celebrity by serving a long prison sentence for refusing to inform on anybody.

Skin the goat also appears in Ulysses, he comes into the story of the last murder. The Irish National Invincible, usually known as 'The Invincible' was a radical splinter group of the Irish Republican Brotherhood and the leading representatives of the Land League movement, both of Ireland and Britain.

This group of assassins were active in Dublin between late 1881-1883, with intent to kill then Chief Secretary 'buckshot' Forster, jurists, informers and likes.

**Edward Evans Death.**
**DATE 6 TH OCTOBER 1965.**

Date Charles Parnell died. 6th October. Synchronized dates again?

First the area that Edward was picked up from.

Central Station, Manchester. This area was where the Peterloo Massacre took place back in 1819, a political uprising in Manchester which resulted in innocent deaths of local workers.

That is a good connection to the Easter uprising 1916. All included in important dates in the British Army's timeline.

The house, in Hattersley, where the murder took place.

Music "It's all over baby blue "Bob Dylan . . . . A record with lyrics which are classed as surrealism. Like Joyce's Ulysses.

The line of the song includes "A Vagabond at your door" Again a link to GREENWICH VILLAGE USA.

Myra goes to pick up David Smith at his home dressed in ragged clothes, not her usual smart dress. Maureen noted that she wore old pumps, a ripped skirt, messy hair and makeup and old jumper; she's acting out the song?

Ulysses now, in the book by James Joyce there is a chapter called Eumaeus. In this chapter there is the member of the Invincibles included. Skin the Goat, (the getaway driver of Joe Brady).

What it says in this chapter is that Bloom dressed as a beggar calls at the hut of Skin the Goat, to come back to the house to sort out Molly's suitor.

Is this too much of a coincidence again?

Asking David Smith to come back to the house in Hattersley to help Brady with the murder of Edward?

He was already on board with the pair to do a robbery the next day. Just as the Invincibles took part in murder, so did they?

I have also noted this . . . many believe that 'Crime and Punishment' comes into the murder. A book relating to a robbery and murder using an axe!

Edward was killed with an axe. But I have found that Oscar Wilde and his book A Portrait of Mr WH may be the link here.

Brady has a bookshelf in the house with books, one that would prove to be important holding the ticket to the

Erica Gregory

lockers at the train station, later found by police. But there is also mention of a birdcage in the house.

When Edward was found the next morning, he was trussed up and upstairs, found with his body were yet more books. One book I find important to Art Films. La Dolce Vita.

Oscar Wilde was a homosexual. His book A portrait of Mr W H, begins with this . . . . I had been dining with Erskine in his pretty little house in Birdcage Walk, and we were sitting in the library over our coffee and cigarettes, when the question of literary forgeries happened to turn up in conversation.

So we have a library and a Birdcage mentioned. Also the name of a man, W H.

The story is about a painting of a young man who was an actor, but who Shakespeare had a love for. He wrote sonnets for this man. But this is a description of the painting.

It was a full-length portrait of a young man in late sixteenth-century costume, standing by a table, with his right hand resting on an open book. He seemed about seventeen years of age, and was of quite extraordinary personal beauty, though evidently somewhat effeminate.

One of the Books with the Body of 17 year old Edward.

La Dolce Vita is an Italian Art Film.

La Dolce Vita is a 1960 comedy-drama film written and directed by the critically acclaimed director Federico Fellini.

The film is a story of a passive journalist's week in Rome, and his search for both happiness and love that will never come.

It has a quote which I feel is what Brady was saying with all of this ". . ." Maybe one day we'll all be homosexual.

Another book 'The Red Brain' is a pulp fiction story published in 1965 by Donald Wandrei. This is a science fiction story.

The Red Brain: The end of the universe comes in the form of a great smothering sea of cosmic dust, blotting out stars and suffocating planets. Only Antares is left, with its race of immense brains, which have for centuries devoted their thoughts solely to destroying the cosmic dust, even at the cost of their own destruction. Then the red brain reveals its plan . . .

The Pulp Fiction books are from the 1920s also. Many have stories of Little Green men and lasers. One man in particular is important here. H.P Lovecraft.

Lovecraft was an American author of fantasy, horror, poetry and science fiction. Known for his weird fiction. Another book by this Author is the book of The Necomonicon.

Oscar Wilde was known for his work in Journalism and he was homosexual. He was also sent to prison and this led to his early death. But he also quoted this:-

Oscar Wilde on Crime and Punishment

One is absolutely sickened, not by the crimes that the wicked have committed, but by the punishments that the good have inflicted.

~ Oscar Wilde—(1854-1900)

Things that all seem to mean something? Again acted out to Brady's own work to include Art from all areas. Film, books, music and Joyce again?

He would have used more in the other murders but I can only work from the recourses available to me.

So All the murders now link to something important and all link by dates.

OTHER THINGS WE CAN NOW FIND THAT MEAN SOMETHING FROM JOYCE'S AND BRADY'S WORK.

Westmoreland Street Dublin . . . . Mentioned in Ulysses for a parade that takes place in chapter lestrygonians. This chapter also describes blood of lamb washed by a stream, a good description of our area South maybe??

BRADY

Moves onto Westmoreland Street, off Stockport Road.

Westmoreland is also the area of the Lake Poets in the Lake District.

JOYCE ULYSSES

VIOLENT DEATHS IN THE BOOK

We found a list which is extensive; this book is very violent and descriptive. These are the main ones.

Invincible's in Phoenix Park (political)

- King Hamlet et al (literary)
- Childs; Henry Flower; Bloom of Wexford (local history)
- Rudolph; Mrs Sinico (suicide)

- May Goulding Dedalus; priest and king (symbolic)

- Mrs Maybrick; Jack the Ripper (tabloid)

- Jesus (archetypal)

- alcohol, tobacco (lifestyle)

- birth control (religious)

- hunters, butchers (ethical)

- wars; hangman (statist)

The use of a Poleaxe

Poison including ACONITE and acid in peas? Sulphuric acid in Peas. (on our visit in November the tins we found buried, were pea tins, we have the paper that survived to show this. Also the tins are pre 65 as not aluminium. This was introduced after 65)

Beheading

Knife guns

The use of shoe string . . . The weapon used. Murderer is still at large. Clues. A shoelace

The throwing of a woman into a river He took her to the Dodder/ to teach her how to swim/ He stuffed her nose with cotton wool/ and then he threw her in

The cutting of a throat from ear to ear

SAYINGS

Castration (not a death but included)

Time of the invincible's, murder in the Phoenix Park"

God wants blood victim . . . druids' altars"

The poleaxe to split their skulls open

Slaughter of innocents."

"Down there Emmet was hanged, drawn and quartered. Greasy black rope when they hanged Joe Brady, the invincible

"Decapitated in rapid succession a flock of sheep"

"By virtue of this same shield which was named Killchild."

I seen a man killed in Trieste by an Italian chap. Knife in his back. Knife like that." invincible's . . . plotting that murder all the time"

C is where murder took place."

I don't need to go on with this one, many who know the Moors murders will see what we have here.

## BRADY/HINDLEY

Stated he threw a woman into a river

Above are the ways that the children found were murdered.

The poison one ACONITE is a main Allusion of the book. Blooms father died from taking this. It's also a plant that Witches use to make poison, and is named in the Pagan and Druid books

Aconitum Napellus

Other Names

Monkshood, Wolfsbane, Leopard's Bane, Women's Bane, Devil's Helmet, Blue Rocket

Aconite has a long history of use as a poison, including being used on spears and arrows for hunting or battle. So prolific was it that by the end of the Roman period it was banned, and anyone found growing Aconite could be sentenced to death.

## JOYCE ULYSSES

Mention of the Sacred Heart again in the HADES CHAPTER

Cemetery, sacred heart, the past, the unknown man, the unconscious, heart defect, relics, heartbreak . . . This again is important.

Sacred Heart Flowers for Gods Garden . . . A nun by the name of St. Therese, "the little flower".

Therese saw the seasons as reflecting the seasons of God's love affair with us. St Therese, age 23 She loved flowers and saw herself as the "little flower of Jesus," who gave glory to God by just being her beautiful little self among all the other flowers in God's garden. Because of this beautiful analogy, the title "little flower" remained with St. Therese.

This Nun was of the Sacred Heart and she had a sister called PAULINE. Ian Brady shares his birthday with the Nun of the Sacred Heart.

## BRADY AND HINDLEY

Hindley gave a wreath saying "Another flower for Gods Garden "for the funeral of Angela Dawn. She often quoted that the bodies at the moor were her Flowers in Brady's Garden.

The HADES chapter again.

Something the group did in November 2012 made us realise the Sacred Heart means more. We visited the grave of Michael Higgins in the cemetery at Gorton. When we arrived we found a large statue next to the grave. 'The Sacred Heart Statue'.

## JOYCE ULYSSES

Gold Cup Horse races and betting on the horses

## BRADY/HINDLEY

Something they mentioned as something special to them and winning on the horses and going on a holiday

## JOYCE ULYSSES

The mention of Molly and Blooms characters leaning towards the East, Yorkshire is mentioned, also Richard III and the White Rose.

Adding a few comparisons here that will connect to the suitcase and its contents and also the Plan for Edwards Disposal. The W.H and the fact at the end of these notes for Edward it states NEW STORY?

Mentions of a Halibut oil tin and Jacob's tin.

## BRADY

Used a Halibut oil tin to hide his negatives. Myra also stated that something was buried in a tin on the moors. We don't know if that was ever found, but we hope she meant it was in our area. We will be looking for this also. Stated that Keith was buried in Yorkshire, our area of Greenfield lays on the Yorkshire side. The 'White Rose 'area. The old Boundary lays to the right of the Standing stones in that area.

## JOYCE ULYSSES

Character Milly Bloom based on his daughter Lucia a dancer and photographer. She was close to her father and they would often write to each other and I did find that picnics were mentioned.

## BRADY HINDLEY

Would take a young lady Patty Hodges on picnics and treat her special??? She even has a look of Joyce's daughter.

## JOYCE ULYSSES

The mention of a bookshelf with books in a specific order. One of the books with a white ticket. These books are of all types. Book keeping and clerking, a Thom's Street directory. Star gazing, philosophy, Body strength and mind, Geology amongst many others.

## BRADY

Takes a job as a CLERK, a stock clerk in a chemical factory. (on the 2nd February Joyce's Birthday, Ulysses publication), at the factory he met Myra.

Star Gazing we believe he mapped the area in this way creating his own maps.

Body strength? He would boast that he could carry Myra up over the moor to practise for the murders.

They used a Street Directory which Myra stated was to find people who had abused animals. We now believe this is how he found his victims names and groomed them. By searching a local directory he was able to plot his journey around Manchester. Pick up a victim or groom victims so they trusted them.

The ticket in the book which led police to the suitcases.

## JOYCE ULYSSES AND LIFE

Two men who were to meet with Joyce and involve him in one of the most ludicrous situations in his life a man named Percy Bennett and Henry Carr.

These men were included in the book Ulysses.

## BRADY

P/B and a Carr were also included in Brady's disposal plan for Edward.

This is one reason we now believe W H is a person and that would be EDWARD himself.

Check WH is to check Edwards's grave at the place P/B maybe??? But a STN CARR is on the plans also. And DAVE CARR. Are they Characters?

There are just so many things that are the same we have to be on to something. I have tried to keep on the facts of things which have been written about for you all to understand. But I can see much more from what I have read and re-searched which matter also. By using the pigpen cipher of the Rosicrucian / Freemasons someone with access to the notebooks may be able to see something that has been missed.

## JOYCE

Ulysses, is a ***Roman à clef***, this in French means a Novel with a Key. The fictitious names in the novel represent real people, and the "key" is the relationship between the nonfiction and fiction. Another book written this way is The Carpetbaggers by Harold Robbins, Many books by Henry Miller, along with Peyton Place, Nabokov's Lolita, and Lady Chatterley's Lover by D.H Lawrence.

## BRADY

Carpetbaggers, a book Myra stated in a letter from which Brady took ideas. This book and film both released in 1961, and 1964, have a connection also to the use of the reel to reel tape recorder. This is by the use of the character Jonas "Cord" Lear. Lear was a developer of the 8 reel tape and the reel to reel tape deck. Used by Brady to tape the GREEN tapes. The Books of Henry Millers were in the blue suitcase. I have also found others were on the book shelf in Hattersley. Brady stated to Myra at the trial to, "Remember the Key".

# EPISODE 13

# FOOD FOR THOUGHT

---

DATE 24th APRIL—3RD MAY.

Maureen Hindley was the younger sister of Myra Hindley; she was born when Hindley was the tender age of 4.

Maureen was a happy little girl and had a close relationship with her sister although they lived apart, they did see each other every day.

As Maureen began to reach her teen's she became a concern to her family. The people she was spending time with were classed as troublemakers.

Maureen was seen to be something of a wild child, she began to dress older than she was and started wearing heavy make-up. Maureen was friends with Pauline Reade although they were not what you would class as close, they spoke mainly in passing.

Maureen in her teens started a relationship with David Smith, who had previously been in a relationship with Pauline Reade although not a lot of their relationship is known.

Maureen and David became close and this developed in to a serious relationship. Maureen's parents however did not approve of him even though they knew she was a wild child they believed Smith would drag her further down. He was seen as a low life, a boy not to be associating with.

The Hindley's disapproved so much they refused to attend the couple's shot gun wedding on the 15th August 1964. Although the Hindley's disapproved Myra was happy for her sister. Myra and Ian even took the young couple for a drive to the Lake District the day after the wedding as a kind of Honeymoon present. Ian acting the true gent paid for a boat ride their lunch and all their drinks.

David Smith was a normal kid; he had a fairly troubled childhood but happily settled down with Maureen.

They married and had a baby girl named Angela Dawn. They spent some time socialising with Maureen's sister Myra Hindley and Ian Brady. It was not until the sudden death of their six month old daughter that things started to spiral out of control.

David later said "It was like a huge car crash those few years of my life". Some people believed David Smith had more to do with the murders than he admitted too. Although he was only 14 when Pauline Reade disappeared, why would Brady entrust a 14 year old with such a big secret and responsibility. Also Brady and Smith hardly knew each other at this time.

We have found now Dates are synchronized with events in James Joyce and his life. If this is so then we take a new turn with a date that also meant something to Myra Hindley.

This date Sunday 25th April was the date of the death of Myra's niece, Angela Dawn Smith?. (we have also been given the 23rd but dates here are signficant).

The little girl died of what was believed to be a bronchial infection. David Smith stated he was at work that day. But where ever he was, he was not around at the time this happened.

If we are to believe dates are significant then at this time Brady it seemed would be moving towards a more political period. Creating his own gang and getting Smith on board to plan another murder and a robbery. Did he and Myra use the death of the baby to mark this event?

The Easter uprising of Ireland 1916 date 24th April—3rd May. Patrick Henry Pearse was a teacher who gave support to James Joyce and was included in his book's along with Charles Parnell, Joyce took lessons in Gaelic from him, Pearse was executed on the 3rd May 1916 for his involvement in the Easter uprising.

Another important date here that Brady would remember 25th April Oliver Cromwells Birthday.

In Ulysses there is a chapter "episode" which we believe could be mirrored with her death.

Hades chapter is revolved around a funeral of a friend. But on this day the chapter of Bloom remembers the death of his son Rudy. Molly had wrapped Rudy in a jacket/waist coat for his funeral. The waist coat of a friend in the book is also a symbol of the chapter. In this chapter Bloom takes "Stephen Dedalus back to his house to study and takes him under his wing". During the time of Angela Dawn's death 'Brady had taken David Smith under his wing' had Smith become Brady's student?

During this time he would give Smith books to read, they were of a Sadistic Nature, Including Justine, by the Marquis De Sade.

Joe Brady also comes in to this with the Invincible's. Was Brady now trying to get together his own invincible gang? They had started making plans for a robbery; Brady was probably testing Smith to see how far he would actually go.

Did the death of the little girl now give Brady the opportunity to manipulate Smith?

The flowers Hindley bought for the funeral she wrote on a card "another flower in God's garden". As explained in this book we believe Brady and Hindley had developed their own symbolic gardens on the Moor's. Does the note on the card have a symbolic meaning behind it? Was Myra stating by writing this that the baby was "A flower in Brady's garden"?

Brady, after being in prison for many years, wrote to many journalists. In one letter he quoted (stated in Janus) about, "murdering a baby in its cradle" Colin Wilson believed it was the following poem by William Blake.

*Erica Gregory*

## Poem by William Blake:

The poem is part of 'The Marriage of Heaven and Hell.'

In seed time learn, in harvest teach, and in winter enjoy.
Drive your cart and your plow over the bones of the dead.
The road of excess leads to the palace of wisdom.
Prudence is a rich ugly old maid courted by incapacity.
He who desires but acts not, breeds pestilence.
The cut worm forgives the plow.
Dip him in the river who loves water.
A fool see's not the same tree that a wise man see's,
He whose face gives no light, shall never become a star.
Eternity is in love with the productions of time.
The busy bee has no time for sorrow.
The hours of folly are measur'd by the clock, but of wisdom: no clock can measure.
All wholesome food is caught without a trap or a net.
Bring out number weight and measure in a year of dearth.
No birds soars too high, if he soars with his own wings.
A dead body, revenges not injuries.
The most sublime act is to set another before you.
If the fool would persist in his folly he would become wise.
Folly is the cloak of knavery.
Shame is prides cloak.
Prisons are built with stones of law, brothels with bricks or religion.
The pride of the peacock is the glory of God.
The lust of the goat is the bounty of God.
The wrath of the lion is the wisdom of God.
The nakedness of women is the work of God.
Excess of sorrow laughs, excess of joy weeps.

The roaring of lions, the howling of wolves, the ranging of the stormy sea, and the destructive sword, are the portions of extremely too great for the eye of the man.
The fox condemns the trap, not himself.
Joys impregnate, sorrow bring forth.
Let man wear the felt of a lion, women the fleece of the sheep.
The bird a nest, the spider a web, man friendship.
The selfish smiling fool, and the sullen frowning fool, shall be both thought wise, that they may be arid.
What is now proved was once, only imagined.
The rat, the mouse, the fox, the rabbit: watch the roots;
The lion, the tiger, the horse, the elephant, watch the fruits.
The cistern contains: the fountain overflows.
One thought, fills immensity.
Always be ready to speak your mind, and a base man will avoid you.
Everything possible to be believed is an image of truth.
The eagle never lost so much time, as when he submitted to learn of the crow.
The fox provides for himself, but God provides for the lion.
Think in the morning, act in the noon, eat in the evening, sleep in the night.
He who has suffer'd you to impose on him knows you.
As the plow fellows words, so god rewards prayers.
The tiger of wrath are wiser than the horses of instruction.
Expect poison from the standing water.
You never know what is enough unless you know what is more than enough.
Listen to the fools reproach! it is a kingly title!

The eyes of fire, the nostrils of air, the mouths of water, the beard of earth.
The weak in courage is strong in cunning.
The apple tree never asks the beech how he shall grow, nor the lion, the horse, how he shall take his prey.
The thankful receiver bears a plentiful harvest.
If others had not been foolish, we should be so.
The soul of sweet delight, can never be defil'd.
When thou seest an eagle, thou seest a portion of genius, lift up the head!.
As the caterpillar chooses the fairest leaves to lay her eggs on,
So the priest lays his curse on the fairest joys.
To create a little flower is the labour of ages.
Damn, braces; bless relaxes,
The best wine is the oldest; the best water is the newest.
Prayers plow not! Praises reap not!
Joys laugh not! Sorrows weep not!
The head sublime, the heart pathos, the genitals beauty,
The hands and feet proportion.
As the air to the bird of the sea to a fish, so is contempt to the contemptible.
The crow wish'd everything was black, the owl, that everything was white,
Exuberance is beauty.
If the lion was advised by the fox, he would be cunning.
Improvement makes strait roads, but the crooked roads without improvement, are roads of genius.
Sooner murder an infant in its cradle than nurse unacted desires.
Where man is not nature is barren.
Truth can never been told so as to be understood, and not be believ'd.
Enough! Or too much?

William Blake's work had been quoted by Myra, many times. Blake himself is included in Joyce's work, where he appears as a teacher.

With all we have found linking the death of Angela Dawn we do not believe that he was quoting the poem, but giving cryptic clues. As you can see the poem is quite lengthy and mention's a lot of random things, so why use just the quote about "Murdering a baby in its cradle" why not any other?

Ian Brady knows his poetry so I'm sure that he would have quoted the poem correctly and not used incorrect words. Another connection with this, Brady and Hindley would by gifts after a murder. On the 27th April Myra recieved a new car, and Brady bought a new triumph motorbike with Fairings. Seem like very extravagant gifts, and for what reason.

# EPISODE 14

# THE SOUTH

---

In our opinion, the police and civilians have been searching the wrong area of Saddleworth Moors.

Firstly the police have concentrated on the Wessenden head/Shiny Brook area for several reasons, the disposal plan discovered for Edward Evan's had the initials WH. It read "W/H **check periodically unmoved'** at first the police thought it meant Woodhead, but were later pointed towards Saddleworth Moors.

Secondly, the map drawn by Hindley herself was thought to point to Shiny brook. A description by Brady gave the police clues as to what they would need to look for. Brady and Hindley both stated that lists of landmarks are needed.

The landmarks are;

* A split tree
* A Stream
* A Waterfall
* Remains of Stone sheep pens
* A Weir

*The Secret Key To The Moors Murders*

* Railway Lines
* A Large Rock Around 5ft Tall

If we look at the Shiny Brook area, these landmarks are present, except for the 5ft rock.

We know the police have searched the area and never found it.

However, the area that we are currently searching has a large 5ft rock that stands in an area not far from two waterfalls and a stream bed, (this area is where we found the shovel on the 20th November 2011).

If I describe our area you will see all of the markers Brady quoted for the unfound remaining victim.

Just before the junction with Rimmon Pit Clough, the stream from Holme Moss has a waterfall and the remains of sheep pens.

The two streams then join and slow down to a weir and what was an old railway line, this was used by workers building the reservoirs in the 1800s.

If you sit up high on the plateau over looking Greenfield Brook you can see the remains of a standing stone circle, with the large rock just below.

The area is known as Lamb Knoll, the area has a stone formation, a Druid stone called Lamb stone.

Above this set of rocks we have the Standing Stones, which Brady called his Stonehenge.

Brady stated if he stood on this rock formation he would be able to see all his burial sites, a viewing point from the Standing Stones.

Shiny Brook cannot be seen from here.

I know this for certain because on one of our trips to the Moors Paul, Margaret and I climbed the steep hill to the Standing Stones and checked the view points.

In this area we also have the split tree where on a previous visit we found the bones of the post-mortem cut sheep buried beneath. The bones have been dated to 1962-67 by an anthropologist. Many more items have been found in the area placed and hidden under rocks.

We need to take a look at some of the statements made by Hindley.

She stated Keith went 'like a lamb to the slaughter' a strange statement to make to describe the situation. Why that? Is it a way of describing an area she was indirectly pointing to?

We also have Hindley stating she climbed up to a plateau to check the horizon for shepherds or hikers.

We have spoken to the landowner and he confirmed they would only shepherd their land. So they must of been insight of the farm, this is not possible from Shiny Brook.

Now Hindley gave a statement to Topping when interviewing her about the burial place for Keith.

The following statement has been taken from Topping's autobiography 'I asked her if Ian Brady had marked the grave. She said she found out later where the spot was, when one day they went up there with the dog.

They had taken sandwiches and a bottle of wine and Brady put the wine in the stream to cool. The dog disappeared into a dip and was found sniffing around a dead lamb. Brady kicked the dog away and picked up the lamb and threw it as far as he could. She said, then she knew that this was the place where he had buried Keith Bennett'.

Hindley also stated that while she was sat on the plateau waiting for Brady to arrive back from killing Keith, she thought she heard somebody coming but when she looked it was a sheep.

We do know sheep may have wandered over to the area of Shiny Brook area but it has been indicated by the farmer that it's more likely the sheep and lambs would have been on the farmer's land which includes the Lamb Knoll area.

Now we look at the description of where the shovel was described as being buried, Hindley stated they walked back along the stream and buried the shovel into a shale bank. This is also indicated by Hindley's map she drew for Topping.

On 20th November 2011 we found a shovel.

Within minutes of arriving at the site the metal detector started alarming and when Paul dug into the shale he came across the shovel. The handle had been snapped off.

The shovel was sent by us for forensic testing, this was done as police at Cold case only test for DNA from human remains.

After months of extensive testing, the forensic gave us the shovel back with the report. We now have samples prepared and sealed with the advice that further testing should be carried out.

The shovel is of the right age; it's a grave digging shovel and is not something you would expect to find on the moor.

We have not been told the shovel is the one Brady used, as we have no photos of him holding this, but it has also NOT been ruled out.

The location of the shovel also matches Hindley's map. A simple rotation of her crudely drawn map matches the paths, streams and the shovel.

Now we come to the deeper and more in depth reasons for our search of the area.

Some of this may sound coincidental and made up of theories but as previously stated how many coincidences

*The Secret Key To The Moors Murders*

and theories do people need before they accept we could be right?

Again we need to look at a few things mentioned in interviews by Brady and Hindley.

Hindley stated on several occasions about a Crux, people have always believed this pointed to her previous religions, however the more we look at the Crux the more we see it can relate to the burial positions.

If we look at Dante's Crux we see a position that was meant for Keith. Dante's Crux is a constellation of stars with a possible reference to the southern cross as a group of four stars seen only in the southern hemisphere (it is allegory which means that the characters and images have more than just one meaning). Dante's Crux was found to be link to Keith by Myra's quote of

"Our code was our crux so to speak."

If we look at the burial sites of Pauline, John and Lesley they all are at points of the Crux, Pauline buried in the North, John is placed in the West and Lesley was discovered in the East which leaves south for Keith.

There is also the link from Ulysses that states the sign of a Crux is built from Molly's body;. There is then The Finnegan's Wake link of the compass points, Dante's Crux is also in the shape of a crucifix pointing slightly anti-clockwise. The crucifix, representing Christ, but If you turn the crucifix anti-clockwise it represents the anti Christ and a person being buried in this position is supposed to be refused entry to heaven.

Brady also stated in his book 'The Gates of Janus' that if the police had worked in anti-clockwise they would have found the body by now.

Travelling in an anti-clockwise position also means you meet the devil on your journey.

The Gates of Janus holds many clues' that will direct you to the area of the graves at Saddleworth.

Brady's book is complex and has taken a long time to decipher. But we knew that a serial killer could not write a book about other serial killers without letting slip, something which related to his own crimes.

The title of the book is a clue, 'Janus' is a God of January and has Two Faces, One facing North and the other facing South, he holds the Key to gates and time.

Brady was born in January. The two gates represent Cancer North and Capricorn South. Myra was born under the zodiac sign of Cancer, and Brady a Capricorn.

The Two Gates to which Janus held the key, one being heaven, the other hell!

Now let's look at North, Brady stated that both he and Hindley had their own gardens on Saddleworth Moor, if you keep your garden gate open, metaphorically speaking keeping the gates of Janus open is keeping your gate to Hell open.

Hindley gave Peter Topping the whereabouts of Pauline's body by explaining what she could see that evening.

She could have disclosed the whereabouts of Pauline's body in the 1960's. Had Myra been a victim of Brady's sick games, as she later claimed then surely she would have given this evidence sooner. She and Brady were still keeping the secrets of other children they had murdered. Hindley was no innocent.

Hindley disclosed the location of Pauline's body to Topping in the 1980's after Ian Brady had disclosed there were other bodies on the moor.

We believe the girl's were the 'Flowers' in Myra's garden and the boy's were Brady's.

It would not be Hindley's job to give away the location of the boys; that would be down to Brady.

If Brady closes his 'gate' he would lose his power.

Brady was and probably still is, very anti-Christ and turned Hindley away from her Catholic Belief's.

In late October 2012, The Group met at Gorton Cemetery in Greater Manchester to visit the graves of Pauline Reade and Michael Higgins (Hindley's friend who had drowned).

Brady and Hindley frequently visited Michael's grave so we decided to take a look.

It was actually quite sad to find Michael's grave was so uncared for.

There is no headstone bearing his name and the plot was overgrown with weeds and a dead tree stump.

Lesley kneeled and began clearing his grave. Her feeling was Michael was an innocent and as such felt sorry that his final resting place had been so neglected.

She removed a piece of rotten tree, and as she did noticed a rounded black shape within the hole. Curious as to what this may be Lesley tried to grasp the item to remove it from the soil. It crumbled into pieces, but the shape left in the soil clearly showed the item was a shoe. Placing her hand into the hole she pulled out the crumbled pieces of black leather.

Could this be the missing shoe of John Kilbride?

Samples have been sent to the forensic laboratory for testing but as yet we have no results.

In the bible, St John gives St Michael a pair of shoe's as forgiveness.

Was Hindley giving Michael, John's shoe as a way of asking for forgiveness?

*The Secret Key To The Moors Murders*

She always felt responsible for his death, not being with him that day.

Next to Michael's grave stands a very significant headstone.

This headstone is a very large statue of Christ; it is the sacred heart statue.

Looking at this picture you may be able to see our significance.

The Sacred Heart Statue, the Heart looks like a locket, and two hands missing. The smaller statue at the base not shown. But something is also missing from this. Stands next to Michael Higgins Grave. Is this a map of the Moors?

Firstly, the heart itself resembles a necklace. (Pauline Reade's gold heart locket was taken from her the evening she was murdered).

Then look at the hand's in the West and East positions they are missing.

We know Lesley Ann had one hand missing and John had parts of his hand missing also.

It was speculated the bones had been taken by animals at the time of discovery.

Below the statue is a smaller statue in what we now see as a possible south cave or crag . . .

The Mad Butcher chapter of the 'Gates of Janus' written by Brady, describes murders which involved decapitation and dismemberment of victims.

Have we found a symbol in this statue marking the graves and showing symbols of parts taken from the children? That will only be proven if we do come across a victim in the area we are searching.

# EPISODE 15

# STALYBRIDGE AND WHALY BRIDGE

---

The Creativity of the wall and Letter, in Finnegan's Wake.

The meaning of the wall again refers to death.

The 'wall' is identified with the tip in Finnegan's Wake, and both HCE's and ALP's turning toward the wall signifies a movement toward death.

Brady and Hindley were seen burying by walls in the area, so what if something was taken from the children as a sort of motif, a souvenir of what they had done, a creativity of some sort?

We visited a stone wall in Mottram, having received information from a local resident.

He explained he had witnessed Brady and Hindley by wall in 1963, burying something.

The couple were behaving suspiciously and the witness upon further inspection found bloody rags.

The witness and his father took the rags to the police. The items were logged into the police files, but of course, at this time they did not know who Brady and Hindley were, they were just a man and woman, behaving suspiciously.

It was at a later date he recognised them and informed the police.

He still has the receipt for the rags given to him by the police.

There may be reasons why these areas were chosen.

Brady and Hindley were seen at other walls too in varying locations, we do not know if anything was ever found by these walls.

But if this was tokens of flesh taken from the children, it would now be long gone.

## OLDHAM EDGE

Oldham Edge has a Roman Wall, a strong connection to the Mills and the Industrial Revolution, but is also an area a member of James Joyce's family lived.

Lord Haw-Haw, real name William Joyce.

William Joyce is Britain's most infamous wartime traitor.

Haw-Haw started off his broadcasts with "Germany calling, Germany calling". This was the call sign of a Hamburg radio station which broadcast nightly news bulletins in English to the British people.

Joyce was Irish by blood, American by birth and carried a British passport. He was a member of the Oswald Mosley's British Fascist Party—a political party in Britain that attempted to copy the Nazi party in Germany.

He was captured, and subsequently hanged at Wandsworth Prison on the 3rd January 1946. The hangman was Albert Pierrepoint another local to Manchester.

In 1960 the film 'Hell is a City' was filmed in this area of Manchester.

This film has been talked about as another obsession of Ian Brady's.

The role played by Billie Whitelaw may have been the reason.

She was friends with Samuel Beckett the playwright.

Samuel Beckett being the boyfriend of James Joyce's daughter Lucia, he had also worked with Joyce on Finnegan's Wake.

The film also has a victim, murdered and discarded on the moors above Saddleworth.

## BRADY AND HINDLEY:
## —WALLS/POETS/WRITERS AND POLITICAL CONNETIONS.

Did Brady's knowledge of local history play a part in the mapping of areas? As did James Joyce, in Dublin.

### Mottram

This area is steeped in History, as with other areas Brady visited, The History would be of great interest to him.

We have noticed the areas he visited and the places the children were taken from, have a strong link to Poets, writers and The Peterloo Massacre of 1819 In Manchester.

Mottram has a stone wall, curiously named The Frog in the Wall.

This is a spectacular viewing point to Hattersley.

It's the History; we believe would have interested him.

A resident of Mottram, Sir Edmund Shaa was a goldsmith and Lord Mayor of London in 1482, dying there 20 April 1488.

He appeared as a character in William Shakespeare's play, Richard III.

Richard III is a play which Brady would quote frequently.

Now take a look at the history of the other areas he chose and we see a pattern forming.

Central Station Manchester where Edward was picked up.

Also the suitcases left here.

This area is known for the famous Peterloo Massacre back in 1819

The Peterloo Massacre (or Battle of Peterloo) occurred at St Peter's Field, Manchester, England, on 16 August 1819, when cavalry charged into a crowd of 60,000-80,000 that had gathered to demand the reform of parliamentary representation.

The massacre was given the name Peterloo in ironic comparison to the Battle of Waterloo, which had taken place four years earlier.

700 people were injured, 11 died and this included a woman and a child.

Here we have a poet whose work had been banned from publication at one time or another throughout his life.

The Masque of Anarchy is a political poem written in 1819 by Percy Shelley.

We now turn our attention to Ashton under Lyne. This is where John Kilbride and his family lived.

Hartshead Pike is a hill in Ashton, Greater Manchester; the name is more commonly associated with the monument on its summit. It overlooks Ashton-under-Lyne, Mossley and Oldham.

This tower is the highest viewing point on the area but also has a time capsule of poetry buried beneath it.

This area is also connected to the Peterloo massacre.

Taken from a story of the Peterloo Massacre:-

After an initial period in Ashton Town Hall the Manchester and Salford Yeomanry were stationed for a time at the Ladysmith Barracks at Ashton under Lyne, which was built in the 1840s in response to the growing unrest. Similar barracks were established in the potential Chartist hotspots of Bury and Preston.

We read that Ashton's most famous poet Francis Thompson lived here.

He and his family lived at 226 Stamford Street which is still standing today.

Francis Thompson became a surgeon and travelled to London at the time of the Jack the Ripper murders.

In fact he became a suspect for Jack the Ripper himself. This history would almost certainly have been an important find to Brady. Brady mentions the Ripper murders in Janus.

Francis Thompson's works are held at The Chethams Library and also John Ryland's at the University of Manchester.

Francis Thompson studied an essay by Thomas de Quincey. This essay 'Murder as a fine art' is said to be reason Thompson became a suspect.

Thomas de Quincey lived in Manchester.

That area is mentioned in the final chapter, as we discovered this area has a forgotten missing child.

In Brady's notebook where the name John Kilbride had been written in amongst the names of actors, one name, a 'Jack Polish' cannot be linked to an actual person or actor.

More food for thought, Is this a character created by Brady for Jack the Ripper? After all Jack the Ripper was thought to be Polish.

## ANCOATS

Moving now to the Ancoats area, where Lesley-Ann was taken from a fair on Hulme Hall Lane.

This area also has Historical links to the Peterloo Massacre.

A building named 'The White house' Public house.

The White House was a rare example of Georgian architecture and was quietly unassuming on Great Ancoat's Street.

It was at the White House where one of the first meetings of Manchester radicals took place in 1812 after the meeting was changed at the last-minute from the Elephant which was on nearby Tib Street, due to a tip-off that the Deputy Constable at the time, Joseph Nadin, intended to break up the meeting.

The last-minute change didn't throw the Deputy off the scent, with the aid of the Manchester and Salford Yeomanry and armed with guns and bayonets; they stormed the meeting and subsequently arrested 38 weavers.

They dragged them away from their ale and marched them to the nearby cells.

It was just 7 years later that meetings like this and the injustices felt by the people of Manchester and further afield would finally culminate in the Peterloo Massacre at St. Peter's Fields.

**Whaley Bridge** is a place which Brady and Hindley visited frequently.

Brady told Peter Topping he had wanted to visit the area as part of a 'deal' he drew to go back on the Moors to help locate Keith Bennett.

He stated 'this area' was important to the case.

Taxal Church in the area Brady would visit often. I found a connection to the Rosicrucian and Freemason's once again by looking at the name. A book called The

Taxil Hoax by a Leo Taxil. The first book produced by Taxil after his conversion was a four-volume history of Freemasonry, which contained fictitious eyewitness verifications of their participation in Satanism. With a collaborator who published as "Dr. Karl Hacks," Taxil wrote another book called the *Devil in the Nineteenth Century*, which introduced a new character, Diana Vaughan, a supposed descendant of the Rosicrucain alchemist Thomas vaughan. Topping said the Church at Taxal has markings that would interest a person who was into devil worshipping.

Whaley Bridge is a small town and civil parish in the High Peak district of Derbyshire, England, situated on the River Goyt.

There is evidence of prehistoric activity in the area, including early Bronze Age standing stones, burial sites and the remains of a stone circle.

Whaley Bridge features in the novel The Manchester Man.

The Manchester Man is a novel by the British writer Isabella Banks. It was first published in three volumes in 1876.

The story follows the life of a Manchester resident, Jabez Clegg, during the nineteenth century and his rise to prosperity in the booming industrial city. It depicts a number of real historical events such as the Peterloo Massacre.

Jabez, being somewhat of an unusual name also relates to Saddleworth.

The Jabez Baths was a popular picnic area in the Chew Valley. It's no longer there having become a part of the Dovestones Reservoir.

## SADDLEWORTH/GREENFIELD AREA.

Ammon Wrigley (1862-1946)—antiquarian and poet. Ammon Wrigley gained a great local reputation as a poet in his lifetime and a literary club, the Ammon Wrigley Fellowship, was formed round him. Most of his poetry was written in Standard English and celebrated the delights of the Saddleworth Moors.

He was a major influence on J.J.R. Tolkien.

## **MYRAS ASHES** SCATTERED AT STALYBRIDGE COUNTRY PARK

We continued to look into the local areas and began to see the area of Stalybridge Country Park seems to be mirrored on Finnegan's Wake. Was this area chosen to be like Phoenix Park in Dublin? Could this be why Myra had her Ashes scattered at the park? Was this her final message to Brady?

Finnegan's Wake is a book of riddles and cryptic messages. When we look at the photographs of Hindley and Brady pictured in all seasons by a tree with F.W carved into it, and an area which seems to be the next chapter in a long and complex play or film acted out by two. This is what we find.

In Finnegan's Wake the tree becomes the stone over time, in an evolutionary process of the Avant-garde entering and dominating the mainstream, before becoming itself an element of the past. This evolutionary process extends to the evolution of both human beings and civilisations.

The saying from the book states, 'Till tree from tree, tree among trees, tree over tree become stone to stone, stone between stones, stone under stone for ever'. Even at the end of man, new growth springs forth in the Wakean cycle of regeneration and revolution: 'Lo, improving ages await ye! "In the orchard of the bones".

Accordingly, at the site of sin in Phoenix Park it is often possible to perceive not only the Wellington Monument, but simultaneously the tree of new creativity:

The four/fire leaved tree is a PHOENIX rising from the ashes of the barren park. The ashes it rises from is linked with ALP (The main female character), she is also represented here as an ash tree. New life is impossible without her and the scene or sin of the fall incorporates both HCE and ALP: 'The scene, refreshed, reroused, was never to be forgotten".

Did Brady and Hindley believe in reincarnation? When they died they would be resurrected and come back as maybe the tree or stone that Finnegan's Wake includes? In Joyce's book the theme is just that and Phoenix Park is the area this occurs. To rise from the Ashes like the Phoenix.

To die in the star sign of Scorpio, we have found, is important, to rise like the Phoenix in the East. The Eagle is connected to the Phoenix. Myra died with the star sign of the Scorpio. Would this also mean Brady must also to be the Eagle, and be reunited with her. The Phoenix and the Eagle are conected to the worshipping of Satan.

The Trees meaning is 'The Tree of life'. The FW tree has never been found by police. Maybe the tree was in Stalybridge Country Park? The tree could be some kind of sacrificial tree. So by taking something after each murder and burying it under the FW tree, was this meant to be some kind of resurrection ceremony?. In Finnegans Wake I did find in the chapter of 'Rose' that the skull of Adam is buried in the Phoenix park with a cross.

THE MILLS AT ASHTON

Finnegan's Wake was a book that included the character HCE, which Joyce based upon Charles Parnell, who we have explained was an important politician and a hero to Ireland. But another hero was the man JOE BRADY, who we also explained at the leader of the group The Invincible's.

Here an explanation again, but read who was murdered in the Phoenix park area.

1883: Joe Brady, the first of the Invincible's 14th May.

On this date in 1883, Britain set about the grim work of avenging the assassination of its Irish plenipotentiaries by hanging Joe Brady at Kilmainham Gaol. "He was brought up as a stonemason," the May 15, 1883 London Times recalled of the by-then-hanged man, "of herculean strength, his occupation developing the muscular power of his arms, which told with such terrible effect when he drove the knives into the bodies of his victims."

Those knife-driven bodies belonged to Irish civil servant Thomas Henry Burke (a quisling figure, in the eyes of Irish nationalists) and the English politician Lord Frederick Cavendish, who were jumped while taking a stroll in a Dublin park on May 6, 1882.

The name of Cavendish we will now explain as a good symbol for the death of John Kilbride.

During interviews Brady stated that a knife he used when he took John was thrown into a canal.

Whilst looking into the local History of the Cotton mills and cotton famine, all part of the Industrial revolution, we came upon a mill in Ashton.

Cavendish Mill is a Grade II listed former cotton spinning mill in Ashton-under-Lyne, Greater Manchester, in the United Kingdom. It was built between 1884 and 1885 for the Cavendish Spinning Company by Potts, Pickup & Dixon of Oldham. Cavendish Mill was next to the Ashton Canal.

If we now believe the name Cavendish is important to the story we are connecting. This Cotton Mill next to the canal may just be the area for the symbol of the knife.

Below are list of the Goons Shows for 1963 as stated in Johns Important dates from the list below you can see why the Canal is important to the area of Ashton for the knife which Ian Brady stated he threw the knife after he murdered John.

Again we are linking a history time-line to the area of Manchester and the books and area of Ireland and James Joyce and his works. I will add here whilst talking about the Goons, That Spike Milligan's book that Myra took from a book shelf in prison, Puckoon, is a book about life in 1920s Ireland during the period of the Irish political uprising.

TELEVISION VERSIONS OF GOON SHOWS

The Telegoons (15 min, b/w) (BBC-TV)

October 5 1963 The Ascent Of Mount Everest

October 12 1963 The Lost Colony

October 19 1963 The Fear Of Wages

October 26 1963 Napoleon's Piano

November 2 1963 The Last Tram

November 16 1963 China Story

November 23 1963 The Canal

December 7 1963 The Hastings Flyer

December 14 1963 The Mystery Of The Marie Celeste—Solved!

December 21 1963 The International Christmas Pudding

December 28 1963 The Choking Horror

I would say that we are getting far too many coincidences which may be hitting on new evidence.

I'm also seeing Brady's interest in folklore and local history is really important to him. Could it be what he had created would now include himself and Myra in this section of local folklore characters. Never to be forgotten. Mapped like a journey through time around Manchester and the environs, a time travellers game?

Everything is now making sense to us, so this would mean the four bodies taken to the Moors was a period in the timeline they created to mark something which they were experimenting with.

After the Crux was created, they moved away, into the next period of a journey, I feel that Ian Brady is still trying to get away from that journey, being arrested at the time of Edwards murder has put a stop to him continuing into the next period of time he was creating.

# EPISODE 16

# Other Links

"Man has no right to kill his brother. It is no excuse that he does so in uniform: he only adds the infamy of servitude to the crime of murder".
***Percy Shelley***

---

Travelling by train and James Joyce's books are important.

The Journey by train is nostalgic to Stephen Dedalus, and is mentioned many times in 'The Portrait of the Artist as a young man'.

Examples:—A Portrait of the Artist as a Young Man, by James Joyce . . . . 'And when he closed the flaps the roar was shut off like a train going into a tunnel . . . . It was nice to hear it roar and stop and then roar out of the tunnel again'.

'the little glimmering stations, manned by a few silent sentries'.

Was Brady playing a character from Joyce's life or work, was he acting out the story? Taking everything and using it in real life?

Using History to map areas, using people to play characters, using murders literally, and copying how they were done.

Then synchronising dates to make this all so more real.

**The Epigraph and its meaning.**

Epigraphs are like little appetisers to the great entrée of a story. They illuminate important aspects of the story, and they get us headed in the right direction. In The portrait of An Artist as a Young Man, Stephen Dedalus quotes.

"Et ignotas animum dimittit in artes"—This is taken from Ovid, Metamorphoses, VIII, 18

Meaning "And he sets his mind to unknown arts"

This does indeed refer to Daedalus, whose "unknown arts" refers specifically to the art of flight, his means for escaping the island of Crete. Taken from the Greek Myths.

Brady's Feet facing North and East.

*The Secret Key To The Moors Murders*

Oliver Cromwell statue once stood outside the Exchange Train Station in Manchester. Now in Wythenshawe Park. Look at the feet position?

The Feet position pointing West and South?

## **BRADY.**

During Brady's trial he was handed many books and Ovid is one book Brady seemed particularly pleased with. This is again a Ulysses link.

I can now see this as Brady was hoping to set his mind to the "UNKNOWN ART" which he had created, and at the end of this was hoping to be away from Manchester.

I believe this is why he wanted to live rent free, and the reason he was using Myra to sell photographs of her. Using any means possible to make extra money, so he could free himself.

I have always felt that a suitcase was at a station filled with his clothes and belongings so he could escape after the robbery he had planned for the day after Edward's death.

## Below are the books listed as on the book shelves in the ITHACA chapter of Ulysses.

Catalogue these books.

Thom's Dublin Post Office Directory, 1886. (Used to map his area and also to find character names)

Denis Florence M'Carthy's Poetical Works (copper beechleaf bookmark at p.5).

Shakespeare's Works (dark crimson morocco, goldtooled).

The Useful Ready Reckoner (brown cloth). (This book teaching Stock and Book Keeping)

The Secret History of the Court of Charles II (red cloth, tooled binding). (Oliver Cromwell and the Battle of Worcester 3rd September 1651.)

The Child's Guide (blue cloth).

The Beauties of Killarney (wrappers).

When We Were Boys by William O'Brien M.P. (green cloth, slightly faded, envelope bookmark at p.217).

Thoughts from Spinoza (maroon leather). (Philosophy)

The Story of the Heavens by Sir Robert Ball (blue cloth). (Star Gazing and the use of Astrology, Brady we are sure included)

Ellis's Three Trips to Madagascar (brown cloth, title obliterated).

The Stark-Munro Letters by A. Conan Doyle, property of the City of Dublin Public Library, 106 Capel Street, lent 21 May (Whitsun Eve) 1904, due 4 June 1904, 13 days overdue (black cloth binding, bearing white letternumber ticket). (A White letternumber ticket mentioned?)

Voyages in China by "Viator" (recovered with brown paper, red ink title).

Philosophy of the Talmud (sewn pamphlet).

Lockhart's Life of Napoleon (cover wanting, marginal annotations, minimising victories, aggrandising defeats of the protagonist). (The French Revolutions)

Soll und Haben by Gustav Freytag (black boards, Gothic characters, cigarette coupon bookmark at p.24).

Hozier's History of the Russo-Turkish War (brown cloth, 2 volumes, with gummed label, Garrison Library, Governor's Parade, Gibraltar, on verso of cover).

Laurence Bloomfield in Ireland by William Allingham (second edition, green cloth, gilt trefoil design, previous owner's name on recto of flyleaf erased).

A Handbook of Astronomy (cover, brown leather, detached, 5 plates, antique letterpress long primer, author's footnotes nonpareil, marginal clues brevier, captions small pica).

The Hidden Life of Christ (black boards).

In the Track of the Sun (yellow cloth, titlepage missing, recurrent title intestation). (Mapping?)

Physical Strength and How to Obtain It by Eugen Sandow (red cloth). (The 1920s and body and mind strength)

Short but yet Plain Elements of Geometry written in French by F. Ignat. Pardies and rendered into Englifh by John Harris D.D., London, printed for R. Knaplock at the Bifhop's Head, MDCCXI, with dedicatory epiftle to his worthy friend Charles Cox, efquire, Member of Parliament for the burgh of Southwark and having ink calligraphed statement on the flyleaf certifying that the book was the property of Michael Gallagher, dated this 10th day of May 1822 and requefting the perfon who should find it, if the book should be loft or go aftray, to reftore it to Michael Gallagher, carpenter, Dufery Gate, Ennifcorthy, county Wicklow, the finest place in the world.(taken from Ithaca chapter)

THIS NOW IS VERY IMPORTANT.

The necessity of order, a place for everything and everything in its place: the deficient appreciation of literature possessed by females: the incongruity of an apple incuneated in a tumbler and of an umbrella inclined in a close stool: the insecurity of hiding any secret document behind, beneath or between the pages of a book.

**Secret documents hidden within the books. The bookshelf at Wardle Brook Avenue the police found the tickets to the lockers hidden at the train station. Books from Ulysses used as part of his plans.**

If you take into account many of the books here on the bookshelf, Brady seems to have used them for his plans. The Local Directory to plan his areas and victims. The Ready Reckoner, a book on how to teach yourself book keeping and stock taking. Brady became a stock clerk. The use of esoteric geometry, how to map an area using the stars. How to become fit and strong in the body and mind, like the Herculean Sandow, a Greek model who appeared with the Ziegfeld Follies 1920s. The Book which mentions Oliver Cromwell. Oliver Cromwell's ideas and political views were a major influence on the up rise of the Nazi Party in the 1920s in Germany and Italy. So a link to the Nazi regime for Brady. Mein Kampf, being written again in the 1920s, and banned in many countries. The book on Napoleon, again rebellious and military. Brady obviously has a love for the military in all periods of time. The Stark Munroe letters, this book mentions a white letter number ticket, is this why a ticket to the lockers at the train station ended up in the binding of the book on the bookshelf in Hattersley.

Something else from the Ithaca Chapter. The mention of objects on the mantle piece. So finding a photo of the house I noted objects I feel are part of a mantle piece display important to Brady.

**First the Ithaca chapter.**

What homoerotic objects, other than the candlestick, stood on the mantelpiece?

A timepiece of striated Connemara marble, stopped at the hour of 4.46 a.m. on the 21 March 1896, matrimonial gift of Matthew Dillon: a dwarf tree of glacial arborescence under a transparent bellshade, matrimonial gift of Luke and Caroline Doyle: an embalmed owl, matrimonial gift of Alderman John Hooper.

On the mantle piece display at Wardle Brook Avenue, there were Two Art Deco dancing lady candlesticks. Two Shire or Clydesdale Horses. The Art Deco dancers I believe are in reference to Lucia Joyce who was a Modern Art Dancer of the 1920s. Also dancers of the Ziegfeld Follies.

The cover of Carol Loeb Schloss's Lucia Joyce: To Dance In The Wake is a photograph of its subject, the daughter of James Joyce, costumed for an original improvisation, part of her first solo dance competition in Paris in 1929. Poised at what might have been the beginning of a career in modern dance.

The Clydesdale Horse and Shire horse are important as a factor or the land they helped to plow. Brady spoke of an incident he remembered of a Clydesdale Horse that fell and broke its leg.

The Clydesdale is a breed of draught horse derived from the farm horses of Clydesdale, Scotland, and named after that region.

Clydesdale's were originally bred to carry knights as armour was very heavy. Interesting as well that Cromwell had no military training, his experience as a large landowner gave him a good knowledge of horses. He was Lieutenant General of Horse in the army. Cromwell's Horse as well, was as famous as he,

Charging into battle at the head of his cavalry, Oliver Cromwell was often in the thick of the fighting during the English Civil War.

And in many of those fearsome clashes he would have been astride his war horse Blackjack.

This now thought could be another possible connection. I found this back in the summer of 2012. We did map this to a GPS system and on a large scale takes you to Martello Tower in Dublin (Joyce's home). On a smaller scale could it of been used to place something important to Brady and Hindley. The N/by NW mentions of a position someone is lying, but a mention of the **bridge of the nose** may mean more. Brady stated that Pauline nose was damaged by Myra. If so does the S/SE position be for something not yet found.

In what directions did listener and narrator lie?

Listener, S.E. by E.: Narrator, N.W. by W.: on the 53rd parallel of latitude, N., and 6th meridian of longitude, W.: at an angle of 45° to the terrestrial equator

In what posture?

Listener: reclined semilaterally, left, left hand under head, right leg extended in a straight line and resting on left leg, flexed, in the attitude of Gea-Tellus, fulfilled, recumbent, big with seed. Narrator: reclined laterally, left, with right and left legs flexed, the indexfinger and thumb of the right hand resting on the bridge of the nose, in the attitude depicted in a snapshot photograph made by Percy Apjohn, the child-man weary, the man-child in the womb. (Quoted from Ulysses).

Whilst looking into the area we have a possible site for a vicitim, The Group began to look into names of the area.

Thinking that maybe like James Joyce, Brady was finding areas that fitted to his books, was he able to find areas in Manchester that would be now mapped like Dublin as James Joyce did. Finding that Pauline was just below an area called Broadstone, reading through Joyce's Dublin, there is an area called Broadstone, An area that was the railway station.

Remember here that the three graves of Pauline, John and Lesley are in a triangle of 375 yards between each grave.

(I do feel you need to remember this triangle).

Broadstone is an area of the inner city on North side Dublin, Ireland. The area is triangular, bounded roughly by Phibsborough Road and Constitution Hill to the West, North Circular Road to the North, and Dorset Street and Bolton Street to the South-East.

The North area is where the train station was, now a bus station. The area to the West is known as Constitution Hill, this area overlooks a canal and reservoir. The East is known as Bolton Street.

The area was owned by Midland Great Western Railway Central Station in Manchester, is where Edward Evans was met by Brady. An area he left his notebooks and suitcases was also at this station This station Manchester Central Station was opened by the Cheshire Lines . . . Sheffield and Lincolnshire Railway

(MSLR) and the Midland Railway. Midland railway also built the Midland Hotel near to the station. This area is also part of the Peterloo Massacre. A Battle that took place on Peterfields in Manchester in the early 1800s.

So we have connections to the Industrial Revolution. All areas where Brady visited has some connection to the Cotton Famine and Mills and to the Peterloo Massacre. Local History that seems to be a major interest to Brady.

But now back to the area. If we take where Pauline's grave was found just below an area called Broadstones, and then look at the triangle, we have a similar map of Dublin. West where John Kilbride was buried, over looks the reservoirs and streams that were dug by Irish workers in the area back in the late 1800's. We are also stood in the area which was part of the Famine Road. Just to add, on a map of Dublin is an area called Grey Stones, if we map our area of Greenfield to the children, Grey Stones is in a similar position again. But this doesn't mean that this area is part of the stories for the children, Grey Stones isn't mentioned in the Ulysses book for the 16th June.

Quote found about Ulysses.

To read Ulysses you cannot miss that the Great Irish Potato Famine is to miss this 'All important' key.

We have to now believe that the Famine is very important here. So if Brady has buried the three children found in a North, West, East position, and within the Famine Road then South has to be a very important place to search for Keith. We did after all find the shovel, and cans etc. in this area??.

One thing about Broad Stone in Dublin I did note is that there is a Black Church in the area. This is mentioned in Ulysses.

St. Mary's Chapel of Ease, universally known as the Black Church, was built in 1830 and was designed by John Semple. The nickname is thought to have originated due to the gloom of interior, rather than the Dark-Grey colour of exterior—the building has very thick walls and narrow windows. An interesting feature of the church is that it has no distinct walls or ceilings inside, the interior consisting entirely of a parabolic arch. Legend has it a person walking anti-clockwise with one eyes closed, two or three times around the church at midnight, reciting the 'Hail Mary' backwards will meet the Devil. However it is highly likely that this was merely an old wives tale, created on account of the church being Protestant. The striking building no longer has a religious function and is presently used as office space.

The Black Church is mentioned briefly in the novel Ulysses by James Joyce, in the chapter entitled 'Oxen of the Sun', as the location of one of Bello's many sins: He went through a form of clandestine marriage with at least one woman in the Shadow of the black church. Joyce lived for a few months in Broadstone, At 44 Fontenoy Street, one of the Joyce families many temporary homes around Dublin. He stayed there with his son Giorgio from July to September 1909 and again from October 1909 to June 1910 while trying to set up the first cinema in Dublin.

Walk around the Church ANTI-CLOCKWISE? just as the children were buried in an anti-clockwise way.

SOUTH AREA

We have noted that Lambs seem to mean something for Keith. 'Like a lamb to the slaughter' quoted by Myra many times. In Ulysses Keogh-Bennett boxing match, Keogh the Lamb of Dublin. Lambs Knoll and the Lamb Stone in our area South.

Something else I found a Lamb important is the Jewish Passover.

The Jewish Community in Dublin another area that Joyce wrote about. He included the community in Ulysses. Leopold Bloom being a Jew. But during the potato Famine in Ireland the Jewish Community helped the poor by just being there and spending money and buying from locals.

Many of the Jewish Community were trades people. Tailors and so forth, is this the reason why Ian Brady had a Jewish Tailor?. Many would agree that he was just a Hitler and Nazi lover. I would say that Germany itself meant more to Ian Brady then just the political side. Many poets and writers lived in Germany and travelled to Germany. If Ian Brady loves books as much as I can see with my re-search, I would say that he would be the first to save books not let them burn as Hitler did.

So we have Jerusalem now important. The Jewish as with Leopold Bloom, and also when we look back at the book Compulsion, the book of the 14 year old murdered by two Jewish students Leopold and Loeb, we are starting to get a pattern.

I began to look at our area as from Dublin, Ringsend the South area and the Jewish Community.

But what I did come across now and a very important part of the Industrial Revolution, was the poet and artist William Blake.

James Joyce loved William Blake's work and included him in Ulysses.

*Erica Gregory*

William Blake (28th November 1757-12th August 1827) was an English poet, painter and print-maker. Largely unrecognised during his lifetime, Blake is now considered a seminal figure in the history of the poetry and visual arts of the Romantic Age.

—Blake was influenced by the ideas and ambitions of the French and American Revolutions.

—Blake used illuminated printing for most of his well-known works, including songs of innocence and experience, The Book of Thel, The Marriage of Heaven and Hell, and Jerusalem.

Jerusalem

And did those feet in ancient time
Walk upon England's mountains green?
And was the Holy Lamb of God
On England's Pleasant pastures seen?
And did the Countenance Divine
Shine forth upon our clouded hills?
And was Jerusalem builded (9) here
Among these dark Satanic mills?
Bring me my bow of burning gold;
Bring me my arrows of desire;
Bring me my spear—O clouds, unfold!
Bring me my chariot of fire! (10)
I will not cease from mental fight,
Nor shall my sword sleep in my hand,
Till we have built Jerusalem,
In England's green and pleasant land

Romanticism (or the Romantic Era/period) is an artistic, literacy, and intellectual movement that originated in Europe toward the end of the 18th century and in most areas was as its peak in the approximate period from 1800 to 1850. Partly a reaction to the Industrial Revolution, it was also a revolt against aristocratic social and political norms of the Age of Enlightenment and a reaction against the scientific rationalisation of nature. It was embodied most strongly in the visual arts, music and literature, but had a major impact on historiography, education and the natural sciences. It effects on politics was considerable and complex; while for much of the peak Romantic period it was associated with liberalism and radicalism, in the long term its effect on the growth of nationalism was probably more significant. The Romanticism period included the poets Wordsworth, Bryon and Shelley, these poets were included in the books given to Brady and Hindley at the trial. Blake was also one.

I began to look into Blake's Art and Poetry and found Blake depicted the Satanic Mills he wrote about as Standing Stones, as Stonehenge. We did already know that Brady was obsessed with the stones, and Standing Stones are just above the area of the Lamb Stones. We also found the Famine Road runs in front of these stones in our area also. So are all the graves he and Hindley mapped, within this Famine Road area?.

The 'Dark Satanic Mills' refer to the 'Great Churches'. Stonehenge and other megaliths are featured in Milton, suggesting they may relate to the oppressive power of priest craft in general.

We are mapping this, and the symbol of the triangle as a 375 yard to see if we are working with two Esoteric triangles that join the shovel, tins and glass we found and then to the Lamb Stones, within the line of the Famine Road.

We also found a sad coincidence, if this is what it is. Keith Bennett was taped singing Jerusalem, something which his mother kept . . .Was the music of Jerusalem a symbol of the plans, and this a song that maybe Keith heard playing by the killers if they did know him. Records after all are used all the time. (Coincidence maybe)

Looking into the Industrial Revolution, the next I had to look into of course would be the railways. The Suitcases kept at the train station, the meeting of Edward Evans at a train station. The romance of travel by steam, quoted in Janus.

I found that the main railway line to Sheffield at the time Brady was using the train, was the Midland Railways which ran the Manchester to Sheffield line, via the Woodhead Tunnel. Two of the stations this stopped at were Penistone and Woodhouse.

## Surrealism Art 1920s, Symbolists, Living the books to the exact.

Surrealism has cropped up now much in the re-search. From the Ulysses chapter of Circe and James Joyce, to the music of Bob Dylan, The Goons and Monty Python and now the Art and how it came to be a statement in the 1920s.

Brady has been known to quote Freud, he is an important factor in the surrealism. Surrealism is a cultural movement which began in the early 1920s, and is best known for its visual artworks and writings.

Surrealists feasted on the unconscious. They believed that Freud's theories on dreams, ego, superego and the id opened doors to the authentic self and a truer reality (the "surreal"). Like the Dadaists, they relished the possibilities of chance and spontaneity. Surrealism developed out of the Dada activities during World War I and the most important centre of the movement was Paris. From the 1920s onward, the movement spread around the globe, eventually affecting the visual arts, literature, film, and music of many countries and languages, as well as political thought and practice, philosophy, and social theory. Surrealism works feature the element of surprise, unexpected juxtapositions and non sequitur; however, many Surrealist artists and writers regard their work as an expression of the philosophical movement first and foremost, with the works being an artefact. Leader André Breton was explicit in his assertion that Surrealism was above all a revolutionary movement. Andre Bretons 1924 Surrealism Manifesto is one book I have looked at and find that by reading this I can see Ian Brady. This book in itself seems to be a major influence on his ideals.

What Are the Key Characteristics of Surrealism?

The exploration of the dream and unconsciousness as a valid form of reality, inspired by Sigmund Freud's writings.

A willingness to depict images of perverse sexuality, scatology, decay and violence.

The desire to push against the boundaries of socially acceptable behaviours and traditions in order to discover pure thought and the artist's true nature.

The incorporation of chance and spontaneity.

The influence of revolutionary 19th century poets, such as Charles Baudelaire, Arthur Rimbaud and Isidore Ducasse.

Emphasis on the mysterious, marvellous, mythological and irrational in an effort to make art ambiguous and strange.

Fundamentally, Surrealism gave artists permission to express their most basic drives: hunger, sexuality, anger, fear, dread, ecstasy, and so forth.

Exposing these uncensored feelings as if in a dream still exists in many form of art to this day.

Surrealism is closely linked as well to madness,. The French Surrealists in particular, had hailed a number of mental illnesses as an attempt at a flight from restrictive conventional meaning. That is meaning sacrificed by a group or the mass. One of the mental states singled out is Paranoia. Salvador Dali used this state to project his own work.

The Surrealist techniques include.

Games. Recreational

The game of exquisite Corpse, a word or drawing game. A game invented by the Writers and poets in France during the 1920s.

Also the travel game of Potlatch already explained as a gifting game. In Time-Travellers' Potlatch, each player indicates the *gift* that she/he would present to various historical, mythical, or fictional figures on the occasion of their meeting. The game introduces the *object* into an imaginary relationship that otherwise tends to be defined too superficially by an arbitrary and abstract subjectivity. The object—the *gift*—functions symbolically between the giver (the player, who lives in the present) and the receiver (who dwells in the past, or on another plane of existence). Altering the relationship between the two, the imagined gift constitutes a third term: a catalyst of the future in the form of a crystallization of *desire*. Thus the game opens a new approach, from an unanticipated angle, to all the old and unresolved problems of projection, identification, idealization, fixation, obsession, etc. A Sick parlour game brought to life by the pair who gave gifts after each murder. So if we are taking that each murder is a new story, ie a time travellers game, The Romanticism period for Pauline, Dark Romanticism Gothic for John, The Mythology for Keith and Medievalism for Lesley that will be the four period of literature and poetry and History that they used for their Experimental period that stated in 63 and ended in December 64, like Brady quoted. They moved away then to a different angle or area for another murder to take place.

## TRIPTOGRAPHY

This form of Surrealism uses photography. Its a technique used where a roll of film is used three times (either by the photographer in the spirit of exquisite corpse, three photographers). This cause the exposer of the film to look dream like, surreal. It causes a film to triple expose itself, in such a way that the subject on the film is blurred, or hard to see. The development of the film in itself is an exercise in itself. Brady's love of photography comes in here. We did find that Myra stated that Keith's photos Brady took after the murder, were hard to see, blurred. What was she really stating? was this the form of development used by Brady on many of his photos.

Paranoiac—Critical Method.

This is very interesting indeed. Taking into account recent events at the hearing on the week 17th June, Brady's Doctors stated that Brady was sometimes know to state that he was being targeted or that outside forces were upon him.

This surrealist technique was invented by Salvador Dali. It consists of the artist to provoke a paranoid state of mind. This is fear that The Self is being manipulated, targeted or provoked by others. The result is the deconstruction of the psychological concept of identity. Such that the subjectivity becomes the primary target of the Artwork.

I find this very important that Ian Brady is using surrealism in his life still.

From reading the art of Surrealism and how they would use the Art of mental Health patients, it makes me wonder what Brady actually was doing at the time he was classed as insane and taken to what is now Ashworth Hospital. Was he taking the live's of the people he read about to the extreme. All in the name of Art.

What we now seem to be hitting on is that the Surrealism has been used and lived in the plans, just like the chapter of Circe in James Joyce's novel Ulysses. To take this literally again and to be given permission to depict Art at its most perverse was this what was used as a way of displaying the bodies he buried?. The positions of the bodies found and items left with the bodies state this could be so. Add Symbolism and Surrealism together, and I will try to explain what this is.

Salvador Dali was a Symbolist and Surrealist, as a child he was aggressive and was sent away to live with friends at the age 6 years. Dali was influenced by others work and would live out his fantasies at home. His desire to do the exact opposite of his friends and stamp his uniqueness upon the world sought to precipitate itself in violence. In one such incident, Dali, while walking with a friend, pushed him off of a fifteen foot high bridge onto the rocks below. Further, Dali almost numbed the situation by watching the companions mother take bowls of his blood out of the room and calmly ate a bowl of cherries. Dali's acts of sadism and masochism didn't cease with time. One of his sources of enjoyment was throwing himself down stairs. 'The pain' he said, 'was insignificant, the pleasure was immense'. Pleasure and pain seemed intimately entwined. Dali wanted both. One other childhood incident of note included a wounded bat. It was kept in Dali's wash-house hideaway and stayed there overnight. When Dali returned to it was being devoured by a mass of ants. He impulsively bit into the seething mass delirious with pleasure. Much of the aforementioned is present in Dali's symbolism, for example the crutches, the ants and the cherries. However, Dali's imagery had another culprit—his very own blood. By this I mean his natural circulation—Dali used to stand on his head for substantial periods of time to induce hallucinatory image

Dali was an artist that turned his mind to his Paintings that showed his thinking's. Take Brady and look at the similar patterns in his life, take his troubles and his violent fantasies and instead of ART, he turns to murder, and depicts his work in the notebooks, suitcases, photographs. The way that he dressed, the way he lived and ate and drank. Myra as well, she was a symbol. The hair and makeup, the way she wrote her diaries.

We have looked into this now. The cigarettes WOODBINE, the chocolate bar CRUNCHIE. Take the drinks Drambuie, Wine. The way they would state that they would go to the cinema, and be able to go to the front and were made to sound above everyone else. Take James Joyce's work and the life of the people he read about. The Plans of the murders the dates and how important those dates had to link and chain together events in Joyce's life and works. We seem to have a pattern now of the acting out they did.

Woodbine cigarettes.

I found that the year 1929 comes up with a man called WOODBINE WILLIE. He is mentioned in James Joyce's Finnegan's Wake.

George Studdert Kennedy while he was a chaplain during World War I. Woodbine Willie felt God's heartbeat for people and ministered faithfully, through practical love and through his poetry, to the ordinary soldiers living through 'hell on earth' in the trenches. Woodbine Willie, Geoffrey Anketell Studdert Kennedy (1883-1929), was an Anglican priest-poet with an Irish background. He was given his nickname 'Woodbine Willie' during World War I because of his reputation for giving Woodbine cigarettes along with pastoral and spiritual support to injured and dying soldiers. Woodbine Willie died on the 8th March, a date that may mean something.

A symbol to Joyce and the cigarette. I also found that the Woodbine plant is part of the honeysuckle plant. One that is mentioned in poetry by Chaucer ad Milton and in Shakespeare. Again we have that in Ulysses, Leopold Bloom wears a sprig of Woodbine in the lapel of his oat coloured suit.

FRY'S CRUNCHIE

The Chocolate Bar that Brady bought Hindley along with the cigarettes after one of the murders. The Fry's Crunchie was 1929 also. So the year is the same as Woodbine Willie. Is there again a chain here??. Does this just mean that they lived the 1920s and everything had to be exact. Just as the books on the bookshelf, the symbol of the Suitcases, train journeys etc. They lived in a time warp, a fantasy that Brady created from his books.

## PONDS ANGEL FACE

"Could you bring me a bottle of make-up, it's Pond's Angel Face, shade Golden Rose. If you can't get Golden Rose, Tawny will do". Myra Hindley, letter to her mother.

Myras makeup as used by models and actresses from the 1920s and Vogue Magazines.

## CARTIER WATCH

A gift that Myra recieved after the murder of Pauline Reade. Something she kept for all her life. The Wrist watch first became popular in the 1920s period. Cartier being one of the exotic watches at the time. Somthing that I did find also, which I believe is a major connection, is the French photographer Henri Cartier-Bresson. His life again I feel Brady was uisng. a Bohemain, whose parents were cotton merchants. He used the Box Brownie as a first camera. Worked with the surrealist artists. Read Dostoevsky,Schopenhauer,Rimbaud,Nietzche,Mallarme,Freud,Prost,Joyce,Hegel,Engels and Marx. (Engels and Marx connect to Manchester Chethams Library).

Carried a rifle over his shoulder during his time in the French army. I dont need to say more on this the connections are there.

## FINNEGANS WAKE by *James JOYCE*

Comparisons to Brady.

Finnegan's Wake is a complex book which includes many cryptic riddles. A book, which uses the wall as a place where reproductive organs are placed as a meaning to the creativity of Art.

The Ashplant is an item used by Joyce; both in life and literature. This is compared to a magical wand used by a Shaman. In a dream A Shaman appears to Stephen Dedalus and Bloom the characters in Ulysses.

The Ashplant is also a walking stick made from the wood of the Ash tree.

In Ulysses Stephen Dedalus shouts "Nothung" as he waves the ashplant, this is German for "Needful", but it evokes the magic sword in Wagners Twilight of the Gods Der Ring de Nibelungen. This Opera of The Ring is the story of Ulysses.

Der Ring des Nibelungen (The Ring of the Nibelung) is a cycle of four epic operas by the German composer Richard Wagner (1813-83). The works are based loosely on characters from the Norse sagas and the Nibelungenlied.

Joyce uses Phoenix Park in Dublin as the area of his death and resurrection.

Dublin's Phoenix Park opened in 1747, is the largest city park in the world, comprising more than 1700 acres; parts of it have more in common with an untouched woodland or forest than a city park, and visitors are surprised to see herds of deer roaming as though in the wild.

Phoenix derives from Feenisk which was originally the Irish "Fionn-uisge" (white-water), the name of a spring located there.

The pub owned by the central male figure in the Wake is located across the street from the park, and significant events are interlinked with the resurrection symbolism and events which took place in the park.

In both Ulysses and Finnegan's Wake, Joyce makes considerable use of an event which occurred the year of his birth (1882): the murder of two British officials in charge of Irish affairs by the "Invincible." The Invincible were possibly a group within the Sinn Fein, the organisation that advocated violence in the fight for Irish freedom from the British; in any case, the situation caused difficulties for Charles Parnell, who was striving for independence through political means. Charles Parnell died on the 6th October as did Edward Evans.

## BRADY / HINDLEY

Brady had a special name for an item he owned, was this "Nothung" was it the Ashplant walking stick he owned, to which he had given a special name?

Brady is photographed with an ASHPLANT, the wooden stick he carried.

What I am trying to show is by using the books and noting the quotes the pair stated, you will find they were playing a game, both inside and outside prison. This game continued after their imprisonment. They were still acting out the characters they had become.

## OLIVER CROMWELL . . .

Stated in a previous chapter we mention how the Industrial Revolution and William Blake's Satanic Mills may mean more to the area of the shovel and other finds.

Take the poem 'Jerusalem' by William Blake with mention of the Satanic Mills.

Then, reading the Mad Butcher chapter in 'Janus' you find the description of the Kingsbury Run at night, page 178, "It was at night that the Run and its environs took on the most sinister foreboding cast, like a visual projection of Blake's Dark Satanic Mills".

The description of the Kingsbury run is far too in depth, but also reads as though Brady is reliving the scene from his own memory of the event. It's as though the vision is still clear in his mind.

I will add more in regards to The Mad Butcher later, but it was whilst re-searching the poem of Jerusalem, I noticed that a display of Blake's work could be found at the John Ryland's Library in Manchester. I felt we had to go and visit.

Paul and I went on Tuesday 12th March. I took photos of the display and purchased an information booklet, which I later sent to Brady. By sending items that were linked to my re-search I was again trying to provoke a response.

At the time I wasn't sure of his physical condition, and his eyesight was said to be poor. I didn't know if he would even be able to see the items I had sent.

Whilst in Manchester, we decided to go and re-search the Manchester News articles from the 1960's, looking for more previously unrelated missing children or murders which may now just mean more to this case.

The one date I wanted to look at was the 2nd January 1963. Not only was it Brady's birthday, but this also links to a significant date in James Joyce's book 'The dead'.

I have always felt this date could have been the start, and that maybe the dates I was synchronizing to each murder, would link up, like a chain of events, to take a date and then leave a marker.

We soon found two other child murders in 1963, and also a missing 16 year old girl.

The First happened at Platt Fields Park on the 2nd January.

A young girl, Susan Thomas from the area of the park, was found murdered. She was 9 years Old. We followed her story all month and into February to see what had happened. Nobody was charged with her murder.

A description given by a witness and reported in the Manchester Evening News at the time was 'a young tall dark haired man had been seen in the area'.

The second murder happened in Wythenshawe Park, South of Manchester on the 28th January. This young lady, 12 year old Helen Sternshine was found murdered in the park.

The area was searched, and a local found a bone handle knife 3 miles away in the Woodhouse park area, the police stated it was the murder weapon.

The missing child 16 year old Susan Ormerod disappeared from the Woodhouse park area.

To the best of our knowledge, she has never been found.

I then began researching the park. Wondering if the park connected to anything I had already found, maybe The Peterloo Massacre, the Industrial revolution and the cotton famine?

What we found was quite startling.

Platt Fields Park is a large public park off Wilmslow Road in Rusholme, Manchester, England.

It is home to Platt Hall, and was originally known as the Platt Estate or the Platt Hall Estate. Fallowfield lies to the south and the Wilmslow Road runs along its eastern edge.

*Erica Gregory*

There is a Shakespearean garden located in the Ashfield part of the park in the south east corner it was designed to grow only plants mentioned in Shakespeare's works.

This struck me straight away, the Shakespearean Garden; surely this would have been of interest to Brady?

The Hall itself has a history which not only connects to the Cotton Famine and the Peterloo Massacre, but goes back to the Civil war, and Cromwell.

Platt Hall was the home of the Worsley family for 300 years. Charles Worsley, one of Cromwell's lieutenants and Major General for Lancashire, Cheshire and Derbyshire during the interregnum. Also mention of a Captain Worsley, who resided in Platt Hall, he had led the military at the Peterloo Massacre.

We began to join the pieces of the puzzle, we had, the areas of the children, all of the children were within an area related to the Peterloo Massacre, the military, and the Cotton famine.

But into the mix now came Cromwell?

At The Chethams Library in Manchester, had once stood the statue of Oliver Cromwell, the Library Brady would visit, has a history of the civil war and was used as a prison during this time.

The English Civil War (1642-1651) was a series of armed conflicts and political machinations between Parliamentarians (Roundheads) and Royalists (Cavaliers).

So I looked now at the Wythenshawe murder.

Wythenshawe Hall saw the siege by Cromwell in the winter of 1643.

But the date had to fit in with the books especially the JAMES JOYCE BOOK THE DEAD, that was the reason the 2nd January was important, the Dead by Joyce was completed between the 2nd January and the 6th January 1904.

This book by 'Joyce' was what we believed, to be the beginning of his murderous plans, if this date had been marked with a murder, it would mean we could be right with the rest of what we had linked.

So is James Joyce's book truly the link?

Cromwell it seems IS a part of Joyce's books.

James Joyce's "The Dead" . . . . (The story takes place before Cromwell brings an end to the Civil War, and involves a Romeo and Juliet love story.

So are the two unsolved murders in the Manchester parks a coincidence for this date?

Susan Thomas has been mentioned previously by others researching the Moors Murders.

Maybe now we can tie the loose ends and, bring together the jigsaw that has been attempted by others time and time again.

The bone handle knife found in the park and identified as the murder weapon?

Cromwell's Army would use bone handle knives as part of their kit. These knives were made in Sheffield during the period of Cromwell's life in Manchester.

Was the knife a symbol to Cromwell and his army?

The knife was found on Didcot Street.

Didcot has a train station where the Oliver Cromwell Train would be stationed. Described as a' Train spotter's' haven.

Reading about Cromwell and his life I find Whalybridge, (Mentioned earlier as an area Brady wanted to go back to and stated to Peter Topping).

This area of the lower basin Peak Forest Canal is a historic area, which held Dukinfield Hall. The hall was home to one of Cromwell's' Generals.

The Woodhead Pass in Glossop is another area which links to Cromwell.

Woodhead is also a farm in Cheshire in the area of Winwick where the historical Church of St Oswald's is. This Church was occupied by Cromwell's army at some point.

There are Halls in the area like Clayton Hall, where the family of Lord Byron lived and also Sir Humphrey Chetam, the man who built Chetham's Library.

We can go round the area and find Military and Cromwell connections, and also many places of interest for someone who knows his history, dates and also the poets and writers from which he is able to bring to life in his plans? (Theories I know, we can only say this).

But are these theories bringing in finds previously overlooked?

Maybe Brady would go further a field and see the Battlefield areas?

'The Battle of Worcester'. The 3$^{rd}$ September 1651, Cromwell's most important Battle.

Cotteridge, and the Midlands where Cromwell's army were based.

Cotteridge is an area where we hear rumours a boy age 8 went missing.

We don't have any firm information on him, but it was mentioned that he may have connected at some point to Brady. This is from others reports we have read throughout our research.

I often wondered what date this could have been. This would be the link I need. Maybe Brady's tartan photograph albums hold clues to this area? But this is something we have no access to.

He did visit many areas of interest and he loved to travel to the countryside

Cromwell also is a good comparison to Milton's Satan in Paradise Lost. This book of Milton is quoted in 'Janus'.

The Parallels between Satan in Paradise Lost and Oliver Cromwell.

Satan is sometimes considered to be the protagonist of Paradise Lost, an anti-hero with the intention of corrupting mankind. The first few books of Paradise Lost are devoted to developing Satan's character creating many compelling qualities that make him intriguing to readers.

Throughout Paradise Lost we can see many similarities between the character of Satan and Oliver Cromwell.

Cromwell's strengths were his instinctive ability to lead and train his men and his moral authority. Cromwell was a Lieutenant General of Horse in Manchester's army in 1644 and the success of his cavalry of breaking the ranks of the Royalist cavalry was a major factor in the Parliamentarian victory, demonstrating his abilities as a leader that he shares with Satan.

Both Satan and Cromwell used their leadership skills to attempt to overthrow and rebel against authority. Both rebel in order to create what they believe will be a better society.

In Book One we see Satan and his fellow devils, or fallen angels, in Hell where they have been cast after trying to overthrow God and his angels. Satan wanted freedom from being under Gods rule and wanted to overthrow God in order to create equality for all of the angels. He believed that he deserved to be on equal footing with God and when denied this, rallied other angels to attempt to help him rebel.

Like Satan, Cromwell believed that overthrowing the leader, in his case, King Charles I, was the only way to restore peace to society, England. Cromwell overthrew the English Monarchy and turned England into a republic after the execution of Charles I, an execution that he pushed for believing it was the only way to end the civil wars. However, unlike Satan, Cromwell was successful in his attempts at overthrowing the authorities.

So we have many connections to Cromwell we know that can be connected to others. Cromwell's reputation was often influenced by the rise of fascism in Nazi Germany and in Italy. Something only a person who is knowledgeable on his history would know of.

We also know that Brady read German poetry and books. The Goethe and Schiller we have mentioned being all part of that. Not just Hitler.

Another good connection to Cromwell are the 'witches'.

Myra was I would say half Pagan, half Catholic like her character of Molly Bloom in Ulysses. The Ritual side to the murders would say this is so. Just like Brady being a Celt.

For two years in the mid-1640s, terrifying witch hunts were unleashed on a population already reeling from the first English Civil War. "The whole witchcraft scare in the

1640s started in Stour Valley and ended up coming across to Huntingdonshire. The witch hunts lasted from 1645, just after the Battle of Naseby, to 1647.

An earlier witch trial had a connection to the family of the Huntingdonshire Parliamentarian leader, Oliver Cromwell. Some years before he was born, in the 1590s, three people from War-boys were executed as witches. They were convicted of causing the death by bewitchment of Cromwell's aunt, Lady Susan Cromwell. So witchcraft was a part of Cromwell's history and times.

I hope we have not confused you? This is hard going for us. I have never read history on Cromwell and the Industrial Revolutions and it's only since our investigations of being a Paranormal Group that we started to look into areas we have investigated.

The Peterloo Massacre came about after an investigation in the Manchester Underground Tunnels, back in May 2011.

The Great Northern Warehouse having a history with the cotton Famine and mills in the area. Also the poems by Shelley and the PETERLOO event came up on the night. That was way before we realised we were having connections to the Moors Murders.

Many Halls we have investigated over the years, Like Smithills Hall Bolton, Ordsall Hall, even our local Worsley Old Hall, all have a strong history of the Industrial Revolution and date back to Cromwell times.

These Halls have brought us lots of evidence of paranormal activity.

Many of the EVPS we have make sense in relation to what we are doing and have done on the Moors. Messages and words picked up which connect to the moors case, including names of people involved.

It's been a journey for us, and the paths we have taken all led to one place. 'The Moors Murders'.

This isn't something we intended to be involved in.

I have written to Ian Brady with several of our theories, but at the end of the day, only he can say if any of what we have is right.

**More Comparisons to Ulysses**

The Jewish Tailor Ian Brady hired to make his suits, we may have found in the book of Ulysses. Looking closer at the characters in the book, George Robert Mesias was Bloom's tailor. Leopold Bloom the main character of the book Ulysses used a tailor. Could this be something that may have been included to bring Brady and Hindley's act to life?

The Name

Mesias

This is a surname of several potential origins. The first and possibly most likely is from the word Roman word 'mensa' meaning a table, through the later 3rd century Spanish 'mesa' of the same meaning. It was used in a transferred topographical sense to describe a person who lived on a plateau or flat lands. Another possible origin is from the Latin word 'messis' meaning a harvest, and hence an occupational name for somebody who kept watch over the harvest, to drive off brigands or wild animals. A third possible origin is Hebrew, from the word 'mezer' meaning a knife maker.

MORE COMPARISONS.

The use of Rifle Ranges, and shooting galleries mentioned in the book.

Hindley joined a local Rifle / Gun club. Photographs in the albums show many holding and posing with a military Rifle.

What facilities of transit were desirable? When travelling to the City, use of the train or tram. When country-bound, Velocipedes. a chain-less roadster cycle with side basket. This is a bicycle. Brady used a motorbike.

**The bookshelf.**

Let's take a look at the books on the bookshelves mentioned in the Ithaca chapter of Ulysses.

After finding that Cromwell connected to the mapping of areas in Manchester, including The Platt Fields, Whalybridge, and Wythenshawe Hall.

I went back to the bookshelves to check the books again. This raised even more questions? Book four on the shelf is The Secret History of the Court of Charles II.

I had looked at this when we first found the bookshelves. But please remember this book is so complex, and although other books seemed to mean something, others didn't. That was until our re-search went deeper.

Certain things which Brady quoted and included in 'Janus', make us believe he has been sending clues and hints to people for many years.

Others have felt Brady was more like a character of 'Raskolnikov', from the book 'Crime and Punishment'. I researched 'Dostoevsky' the author.

Brady also claimed to be like the fictional character in this book, well 'yes' he killed someone with an axe, but we feel that's not what Brady had meant.

Already finding the Industrial Revolution, The Peterloo Massacre, The Civil war and Napoleon are cropping more than I first realised.

I find Dostoevsky taking me, on a train journey, and onto Revolutionary characters.

Raskolnikov, being just one Character, but there are more.

There are Mentions of Goethe and the French Revolution. This is what led me to the next pathway.

Basically and as simply as I can explain this, the Characters are standing at a train station waiting for the train to arrive to take them on a journey, as one journey ends another begins. One dream is punctured by the touch of reality: it collapses—and there arises a new dream of a new turn around the corner. One train has left the station meaning that character has ended, then one waits for the next one to begin, but a railroad station nevertheless remains a railroad station, a place of transit.

So is Brady looking at his life like a train journey?

It's the revolutions and mention of the bourgeois society of Western Europe. I find are also mentioned in the works of Joyce. Along with Napoleon and Cromwell as books on the bookshelf.

So I began to look into the French Revolution and this period of time in Paris.

In A Portrait of the Artist as a Young Man, Joyce explicitly identifies the markers of bourgeois nationalism. Stephen Dedalus is also compared to a revolutionary. Reading books by Rimbaud a French revolutionary poet, the spirit of Ireland is embodied in young Stephen Dedalus, to rise above the turbulent Ireland of the early 1900s in a rebellion against society. Something we all know Brady was doing at the time was rebelling against society, and Myra was following him, even taking a course on Revolutions in prison.

The area of Paris where the French Revolution took place is the area known for its Bohemian Culture.

The Shakespeare and co bookshop owned by Sylvia Beach is to be found here. This bookshop was known for literature which had been banned and one time or another in many countries.

Bohemianism is the practice of an unconventional lifestyle, often in the company of like-minded people, with few permanent ties, involving musical, artistic, or literary pursuits. In this context, Bohemians may be wanderers, adventurers, or vagabonds.

An area renowned for the Bohemian life style is Greenwich Village. We already have links to Greenwich Village from the Records used as a 'code' and part of the plans.

Montmartre and Montparnasse in Paris are areas known for The Shakespeare and Co Bookshop Ulysses was published here.

Henry Miller and others like Dali, James Joyce, Ezra Pound, Hemmingway and many other Artists lived at one time or another in this area, and also at Mitte in Berlin Germany.

Henry Miller wrote some of books in Brady's suitcases, found at the train station by police. The books were amongst others which I have looked into also.

The Symbolism of free love, a Bohemian lifestyle, is the subject of some of the books which James Joyce had on his bookshelf at home. Another, written by Sylvia Beach, she was a friend of James Joyce.

So we have a Bohemian in Brady and now Hindley as well.

There are two elements; at least, that are essential to Bohemianism.

The first is devotion or addiction to one or more of the Seven Arts; the other is poverty. In modern times liberal arts education is a term which can be interpreted in different ways. It can refer to certain areas of literature, languages, philosophy, history, mathematics, psychology, and science. In other areas, this also includes music, Art, Geography, Humanities and astronomy/astrology. These have been studied by both in prison where Myra got her degree in some.

Then I found this . . . This was now leading me to Brady himself. Thinking about how Brady would dress, how smart he was, and how he tried to be better than his associates.

Dandy: no money, but try to appear as if they have it by buying and displaying expensive or rare items—such as brands of alcohol.

Maxwell Bodenheim, an American poet and novelist, was known as the King of Greenwich Village Bohemians during the 1920s and his writing brought him international fame during the Jazz Age.

In the twentieth century United States, the bohemian impulse was famously seen in the 1940s hipsters, the 1950s Beat generation (exemplified by writers such as William S. Burroughs, Allen Ginsberg, Jack Kerouac, and Lawrence Ferlinghetti), the much more widespread 1960s counterculture, and 1970s hippies.

The word Dandy or Dandyism.

Dandy (also known as a beau or gallant) is a man who places particular importance upon physical appearance, refined language, and leisurely hobbies, pursued with the appearance of nonchalance in a cult of self. Historically, especially in late 18th-and early 19th-century Britain, a dandy, who was self-made, often strove to imitate an aristocratic lifestyle despite coming from a middle-class background.

In 1836 Thomas Carlyle wrote:

A Dandy is a clothes-wearing Man, a Man whose trade, office and existence consists in the wearing of Clothes.

The beginnings of dandyism in France were bound up with the politics of the French revolution; the initial stage of dandyism, the gilded youth, was a political statement of dressing in an aristocratic style in order to distinguish its members from the sans-culottes.

The Bourgeois society. In the latter 19th century, this fancy-dress bohemianism was a major influence on the Symbolist movement in French literature.

So was I now hitting on a profile of Brady as a dresser? People who were classed as a Dandy and characters from books include: Oscar Wilde, Dracula, Dorian Grey, Lord Byron, Montparnasse from Les Misérables and Characters in Dickens books. There were many.

Rimbaud came up again, a 17 year old rebel poet from France. He wears a dandy's cravat and a shabby suit. His expression—with its insolent pout and vacant, sociopathic stare—cannot obscure the feminine delicacy of his nose and the soft curve of his boyish cheeks. He was also a rebel poet and a drinker of something that I now found could be a very good link to the Green Mist that Brady often said he saw. The Green that I thought was Ireland. But now just may be this is the drink ABSINTHE.

**ABSINTHE**. Aka. THE GREEN FAIRY OF DUBLIN.

ABSINTHE used by the poets as a Mind Opener.

I have found links which point to the notion; Brady may have been experimenting with this drink at the time of the murders.

If this is so, Brady would have Hallucinations. Visions and violence are known to happen to some who drink this, Brady often stated he saw a green mist, and had incidents where he saw death???, Being drawn to the Green. Absinthe is historically described as a distilled, highly alcoholic beverage. It is an anise-flavoured spirit derived from botanicals; including the flowers and leaves of Artemisia absinthium (a.k.a. "grand wormwood)

Absinthe traditionally has a natural green colour but may also be colourless. It is commonly referred to in historical literature as "la fée verte" (the green fairy). Absinthe has always been associated with violent crimes of some kind it was also known to give an open mind to poets and artists so they could be more creative. Famous artists such as Van Gogh, Manet and Picasso featured the green fairy in their paintings and poets such as Rimbaud, Verlaine and Baudelaire made it a subject of their writings.

The following are all excerpts from the book "Wormwood; A Drama of Paris" (1890).

I am the green fairy
"I am the green Fairy"
My robe is the colour of despair
I have nothing in common with the fairies of the past
What I need is blood, red and hot,
The palpitating flesh of my victims
Alone, I will kill France, the present is dead,
Vive the future . . .
But me, I kill the future and in family I destroy
The love of country, courage, honour,
I am the purveyor of hell, penitentiaries, hospitals.
Who am I finally?
I am the instigator of crime
I am ruin and sorrow
I am shame
I am dishonour
I am death
I am Absinthe"
Let me be mad!
Let me be mad, mad with the madness of Absinthe

The wildest, most luxurious madness in the world.
Let me be mad, mad with the madness of Absinthe
Give me the fairest youth that ever gladened his mothers heart
Let me be mad
Let him be hero, saint, poet—whatever you will
Let me make of him an Absintheur.
And from hero he shall change to coward
From saint to libertine
From poet to brute.
You doubt me?
Come then—to Paris.

Stephen Dedalus would drink ABSINTHE in Ulysses and this is what is said to bring in the surreal feelings of the Circe chapter.

Would Brady and Hindley again take what is in the book and bring this to life. A very important drink used by the poets Brady quotes from in Janus.

Drinking absinthe, it seems, does have the perplexing effect of "illuminating the mind", as one French doctor put when writing, in 1872, of the transformations the mind undergoes under the Green Fairy's influence. The doctor was especially intrigued by the odd absinthe phenomenon of enhancement in sensory perception. Rather than dulling one's senses, as would be expected from a drink so high in alcohol, absinthe has the opposite effect. The doctor wrote:

"The most curious thing about the transformation of the sensorial apparatus—the phenomenon, at least, which struck me most forcibly in the experiments I conducted on myself—is that all sensations are perceived by all senses at once. My own impression is that I am breathing sounds and hearing colours, that scents produce a sensation of lightness or of weight, roughness or smoothness, as if I were touching them with my fingers."

Did Brady use Absinthe to be creative with his 'ART' so to speak? or was this used to bring the chapters in Ulysses to life and maybe given to the children at one point. After all they did ply the children with alcohol.

Quote from The Gates of Janus 2001 page 111, written by Ian Brady

"All aspects of the serial killers case must be exhaustively studied-family and educational background, pathology reports, police interviews, trial transcript how he spends his time in prison, what he READS, other hobbies, BRAND OF CIGARETTE, FAVOURITE CHOCOLATE BAR, relationships with guards and prisoners . . . . essentially you must read him BY HIS ACTIONS. Much more will revealed obliquely in relaxed, free flowing conversation, touching upon politics, general philosophy topical social questions, AUTHORS, FILMS, CONTROVERSIAL PERSONALITIES, universal moral dilemmas."

There are clues in 'Janus'

Many people received letters after the publication of 'Janus' usually ended with a reference to book.

He stated the book 'testifies' something even on a letter to Mrs Johnson which can be found publically on the internet.

A psychic medium Christine Hamlett—Walsh and friend of Winnie also wrote to Brady in 2005 under the pseudonym of Ms Stockhall-Shaw. Brady replied and also double barrelled his signature.

The letter came with a P.S.

"One reviewer described Janus as the most dangerous book written in the past sixty years. I certainly hope that turns out to be the case, if readers correctly grasp the activism advocated".

Even then he was trying to get people to grasp what he was stating in his book.

Look at the quotes of poetry and literature. They are written with purpose. Each of them being a clue.

Read the chapters through the eyes of Brady. Play his game, and read between the lines. I had to learn and educate myself on subjects I had no previous interest in.

It has taken a year of hard work and dedication from me and the group, to show this.

All we want are the victims to be found or put to rest.

## THE OTHERS

Having visited the reference libraries in Manchester, and spending many hours scanning the microfilm records of newspaper articles of the 1960's not only did we learn more in regards to the actual known moors victims, we also discovered many stories relating to other missing children. Some of whom we covered in the Cromwell Episode.

We noted several names of missing persons.

How many of these other murders are still waiting to be solved? How many could be other victims of Brady and Hindley?

New to the case and with little knowledge we had to start right at the beginning.

Very early on we decided to dismiss Hindley's account of the crimes. Her confessions, letters, diaries and interviews struck us as being a 'Mills and Boon' account of what had really taken place. She may have been able to pull the wool over many others eyes, but not ours.

Her version of events changed so many times. We felt this was simply, because she was lying.

Brady's version hasn't really ever altered. Could this be because he was closer to the truth? After all you don't need a good memory to recall the truth.

Brady's interviews, obsessions with books, poetry and film are the things which should have been taken more seriously.

His constant quotes, to and from Myra, should of been listened to.

The letters they wrote to each other have so many clues, in a language they both created as their 'key'.

We believe all notes and letters containing the work of Wordsworth, were written in code and relate to the murder of Pauline Reade. The work of Shelley pertains to the murder of John Kilbride. Tennyson was their code for Keith, and Chaucer to Lesley Ann Downey.

These letters need to be looked at again.

James Joyce mapped his stories from the areas of Dublin.

Using the local street directory, to find locations, names and places with an importance of history. Dates, people he knew and then using what he loved. Poetry: Wordsworth, Dante, Shelley, Blake, Oscar Wilde, Goethe, also politics, Myths, legends, music and religion.

Oliver Cromwell is mentioned in many of Joyce's books as is Shakespeare.

Anyone who knows the case will see Shakespeare is a major connection;

Brady quotes Shakespeare frequently a favourite being Richard III.

Myra Hindley was also acting out the characters from the books, and fooling many in prison.

Wordsworth for example wrote the poem Tintern Abbey on the 13th July.

Myra quoted his work along with Shakespeare to Brady in a letter. (Their code for Pauline Reade).

Pauline was not known as a victim of the moors for many years, nor was Keith.

So by using the poets as a key in their letters they were playing a sick game right under the noses of the prison staff and psychologists. They were talking to each other about the TWO murders and nobody had a clue.

Any letters that mention Tennyson (Ulysses) or Ovid could well be taking about Keith.

I have no access to these letters but would ask that anyone with access to them please re examine them. If the letters do indeed contain what I suspect then I would be happy to assist the police and the cold case team to see if this sheds any new light on the case.

Looking now at the missing 'others', I won't add some of the names, just the places they were taken and the reason we believe they could be the forgotten other child victims of Brady and Hindley.

We have always felt that the start of the killings would have been 1963. Talking into account our James Joyce connections and comparisons.

At the library we looked into the whole period of 1963-1965, specifically other missing children.

We find a boy age 14 missing from Clayton.

Clayton Hall is said to be a place where Oliver Cromwell and his army stayed. This hall is also once home to the owner of Chetham's Library in Manchester,

Chethams Library is the one place Ian Brady did visit. Many of the poets and writers from the Manchester area and environs have work here. It is also a place where politics is very important. The German industrialist and Marxist philosopher Friedrich Engels lived in Manchester in the early 1840s.Karl Marx, who lived in London, was a frequent visitor to Manchester, and in the summer of 1845 he and Engels developed the habit of studying together at the table in the alcove of the Reading Room. The desk and alcove remain unaltered. The books which the two men studied are still held by the Library.

So Clayton an area Brady would have visited?.

Then we find a 12 year old girl missing from her home, in Shakespeare Street, Chorlton-on-Medlock.

We have no dates for these children, as the article was small and stated "Still Missing", we are not sure if these are solved.

If they remain un-solved, they just may be 'other' victims of Brady and Hindley for the reason the areas have an important history that could well have been marked by a murder. This area has a connection to Thomas de Quincey. De Quincey was born at 86 Cross Street. His father was a successful merchant with an interest in literature who died when he was quite young. The family lived at Greenheys, a large country house in Chorlton-on-Medlock near Manchester. De Quincey wrote an essay on "Murder considered as one of the fine arts"...

He was also an influence on a poet from Ashton, the area of John Kilbride. A Francis Thompson, This poet was a suspect for the Jack the Ripper Murders. Francis Thompson read De Quincey's work, and this had a major impact on his life. So take this into account that the Jack the Ripper murders just may have been re-searched by Brady for ideas also.

On to the next we find a report of an attempted abduction of a young girl., this girl escaped. Ayleen Birch of Coverdale Street in Ardwick was attacked by a man and reported the crime to police. This area is known for its links to Oliver Cromwell, another General lived here from the BIRCH family. I thought it must be a coincidence the girls name is the same. That was until I looked into the Coverdale Street name.

This is the name of a famous bible, The Coverdale Bible, written by a Myles Coverdale, in 1539. The protestant Bible was used by both Oliver Cromwell and Shakespeare.

Ardwick is also the area Edward Evans lived.

So did Brady go back to groom another victim, as Brady has always stated, he knew Edward Evans.

Have we got a serial killer that not only lived a historical time travel, but literally brought it all to life?

Everything he did was taken from what he read, from the films he watched, and from the lives of others.

He then created a world of being in character and got Myra to do the same.

Not only did they do this on the outside but also inside prison. They stayed in character!

Is Brady still doing this to confuse all around him?

If we had access to photos and his notebooks I'm sure I could find all the evidence needed to support our theory.

We have to leave this as open to questions for now . . .

However, we must question if the Moors Murders are possibly just a part of a much bigger picture? The forgotten 'Other' murders, victims and missing children in areas they visited have to be taken into account.

Keith Bennett may not be the only victim still missing.

If Brady and Hindley are not involved in any of the missing and unsolved murders above, then we have two murderers in Manchester at the same time. Who coincidentally were mapping areas that also link to the Arts and history Brady also used in the other areas.

Is all we have found one massive coincidence?

We will continue to help as much as we can to get the truth out. To help not just the victims we know of, but also the ones forgotten or not yet known.

# EPISODE 17

# CONCLUSION AND 'THE GATES OF JANUS'.

"Behaviour is the mirror in which everyone shows their image"

Wolfgang Goethe
(German writer, poet and politician).

---

What we seem to have in the above are connections to surrealism and James Joyce's work and life.

It's not so much the works of these people which led me to how Brady was influenced. It was the lives of each of them.

Each one had themselves been influenced by others work.

People like Henry Miller, whose books Brady added to the suitcases. His life of a Bohemian in Paris, along with Joyce, Hemmingway, Dali and many others, I can see included in Brady's life. The Marquis DE Sade's life was not all about his sadistic side. He was a revolutionary, who spent time in prison for his political beliefs. De Sade had a love of dogs and he would change wigs to suit his mood (here we see Myra).

There is also the writer Nabokov, not only a writer and translator of Crime and punishment, one of Brady's favourite books which he states is important. But Nabokov was also a chess expert who wrote books on chess strategies, he lived in Ithaca in the USA.

This again is a link to James Joyce. Ithaca is the chapter in Ulysses that holds the key to the bookshelf and much more. Nabokov drew a map of Blooms day. This map, a crude drawing, pinpoints areas where events happen on the 16Th June in Dublin. He taught his pupils who worked with Ulysses to map their work in the same way.

The Gates of Janus is also a kind of map taking the reader on a journey through others work, i.e. The first half Brady gives the reader clues on how to understand a serial killer out. The second half is one chapter after another on infamous serial killers.

We find the life of Brady included in snippets and underlying messages.

The chapter The Mad Butcher of the Kings-bury run, seems to describe the area we are searching and the South. Remember the links to James Joyce and the Greek Myths for the 16Th June.

MAD BUTCHER OF THE KINGSBURY RUN.

By taking the quotes of the poets and writers in The Mad Butcher chapter of the Gates of Janus, I have been able to connect to Ulysses and again the 16Th June.

I found the Mad Butcher chapter was very descriptive. Too descriptive for someone who had never been there? Brady quotes that the fog runs down the gully like the River Styx. I found this to be a bit strange, so decided to look at the River Styx.

It's The River of which many know its name, without knowing its origin or what it really stood for. It's a river which separates the world of the living from the world of the dead. Styx it is said winds around Hades (hell or the underworld are other names) nine times. Its name comes from the Greek word *stugein* which means hate, Styx, the river of hate. This river was so respected by the gods of Greek mythology they would take life binding oaths just by mentioning its name. There are five rivers that separate Hades from the world of the living.

It is thought that Charon, an old ferry man who ferries the dead onto the underworld, crosses the river Styx where a dragon tailed dog guards, allowing all souls to enter but none to leave. Also while on this subject, Charon only takes the souls across that are buried properly with a coin (called an obol) that was placed in their mouths upon burial.

This River takes us to Hades and the Underworld.

The Sheep bones we found, placed under the split tree, are a sacrifice to the Underworld in the Greek Mythological story of Ulysses. The Oak tree is the door to the Underworld. We already have the South as Brady's purgatory, or Hell. So finding this mentioned by Brady adds strength that we may just be right?

I carried on with the quotes from the Mad Butcher. Brady quotes William Blake's Satanic Mills, we have already mentioned.

I had yet to look at was the Cleveland Murders of the Mad Butcher and the mentions of Lake Erie.

In the area of Lake Erie we came upon Buffalo.

Buffalo lies at the top of the Lake. The University of Buffalo celebrates Blooms day, the 16Th June celebration of the book Ulysses.

One of the world's greatest literary treasures resides at the University at Buffalo **The James Joyce Collection**. Comprising more than 10,000 pages of the author's working papers, notebooks, manuscripts, photographs, correspondence, portraits, publishing records, important memorabilia and ephemeral material, as well as Joyce's private library and the complete body of significant Joyce criticism, the collection distinguishes the university as the leading resource for Joyce scholarship.

Is this Coincidence again? Or are we meant to be led here by Brady.

Another quote here in the Mad Butcher chapter takes us to Bleak House by Charles Dickens. Why mention this also. Again I looked up Bleak House. The main Character from Bleak House is Esther. Esther in the book buries a doll under a tree. Myra Hindley's first name was Esther. Is Brady leading us to find something under a tree in the area?

This chapter not only describes the area we are in, but is descriptive with the murders. There are things in this chapter we feel may have been directing us to what happened to Keith and the other victims.

The names John and Edward are in the chapter. But it's the fact the area of the Mad Butcher in the USA also matches things we have found in James Joyce's life and works.

The Poet: W H Auden.

His poem of 'The Two' is quoted in the last chapter of Janus.

This poem, as we stated in the time line to our work, led us to the area we are in.

But W H Auden's life may also have been of interest to Brady. Auden was born in York, so a Yorkshire man.

Auden's father, a mythologist was a major influence on his poetry.

Auden's lecturer at University was no other than JJ R Tolkien.

Tolkien was a cryptologist and worked at Bletchley House during WWII.

Auden loved the landscape and moved to the USA where he taught his work to students at GREENFIELD.

The area of Greenfield has a poet's corner, a tower on a hill in the South.

Auden moved to Germany before the 2nd world war so he could live an alter-ego lifestyle at Mitte in Berlin. Being homo-sexual, he was not allowed to show this in the UK, a crime still in that period of time. Mitte is one area where a Bohemian lifestyle was undertaken by many writers and poets and Artists, just as in Paris and Greenwich Village in the USA. So again we have a poet and his lifestyle I feel Brady craved.

### The Two by *W H Auden*

You are the town and we are the clock.

We are the guardians of the gate in the rock.

The Two.

On your left and on your right

In the day and in the night,

We are watching you.

Wiser not to ask just what has occurred

To them who disobeyed our word;

To those

We were the whirlpool, we were the reef,

We were the formal nightmare, grief

And the unlucky rose.


An Analysis of this poem brings in The Greek Myth again of Ulysses, within the lines of the whirlpool. Greenfield is the area we are in.

It's been a very complex journey trying to get these cryptic messages out of a book; things are still coming from this. Hopefully we will get that X marks the spot by taking this further.

What we are trying to show is we have enough evidence to state that something has happened in that area.

Brady's book leads to this area. The area needs to be looked at properly to dismiss it from the search

The aim of our book is about getting the physical help and support we need to bring this to an end.

The police are unable to help us search.

The families want closure.

This is why we have spent so long doing this in a hope others will also see the southern spot should be properly searched.

We do know from a source that Ian Brady has no objection to our book. The source also informs us Brady stated he doesn't know of W H Auden and feels it sounds like a pop song?

Yet he quotes him in 'The Gates of Janus'?.

I would like to finish with a quote.

This is a good explanation of how we see Brady

> "I also paint, draw, and I'm into film and photography, and the same applies to all of them. Your presenting the material to the public and hoping they're going to get what you're doing, some don't, some do" . . .

Paul Kane. Hell raiser movies.

We are continuing to uncover evidence at the time of writing this book.

Written by Erica Gregory and Jemma Leicester with support from Lesley McCormack and Tracy Reed—Goodehall, without whom none of this would be possible.

Copyright owned by the group.

Photos taken are our own taken from the sites we have visited and from public photographs which have no copyright

You can find us on Face Book, Twitter and You Tube. The Secret Key To The Moors Murders page and Worsley Paranormal Group.

Made in the USA
Columbia, SC
07 April 2022